# WHITE EAGLE ON
# REINCARNATION

## *Also by White Eagle*

# *White Eagle*

## *on*

# REINCARNATION

WHITE EAGLE PUBLISHING TRUST

NEW LANDS · LISS · HAMPSHIRE · ENGLAND

First published August 2006

© The White Eagle Publishing Trust, 2006

*British Library Cataloguing-in-Publication Data*
A catalogue record for this book is available
from the British Library

ISBN 978-0-85487-172-8

Typeset in 12 on 15pt Baskerville at the Publishers
and printed in China by Artical Printing

# Contents

# Introduction

WHITE EAGLE'S teaching on reincarnation is profound. He does not deal merely with the fact of rebirth, but explains how this is one of the fundamental elements of life and soul growth.

White Eagle refers to reincarnation as a 'law', and, as will be seen from the contents list, that 'law' explains many of the conundrums of life—why we feel a sense of recognition of some people; why we are drawn to certain countries; why some people seem to be born with incredible skills.

At the same time as explaining these, White Eagle also helps us to understand better how the law of re-incarnation works with regard to animals, families and groups, our own conditions and personalities and the ultimate purpose of our lives.

This book is a compilation from the many talks on the subject given through Grace Cooke (White Eagle's channel) over the decades. Light editing has always been necessary, to achieve consistency, inclusiveness and flow, and to remove anachronisms. Readers should not feel that it is essential to follow the book through sequentially; it will also serve well as an anthology, a book to dip into for teaching about reincarnation.

It may also be helpful to the reader to study this

book alongside another, by Grace Cooke, entitled MEMORIES OF REINCARNATION (republished 2006 by the White Eagle Publishing Trust and previously entitled THE ILLUMINED ONES). This book comprises Grace Cooke's memories of some of her own previous incarnations, in particular, showing how a soul develops and grows throughout successive lifetimes.

WHITE EAGLE ON REINCARNATION is the sixth compilation in the WHITE EAGLE ON.... and completes the series on the great laws begun in WHITE EAGLE ON LIVING IN HARMONY.

Biblical quotations are given in italics and there are references to them at the end of the book.

# PART I

# UNDERSTANDING REINCARNATION

# Chapter One

## *The Wheel of Rebirth*

OUR SUBJECT is the Wheel of Rebirth. We will first outline the picture very simply, because there is much confusion concerning this great principle. Some people feel reluctance or repugnance at the thought of having to reincarnate in a physical body. They cannot understand why, once having passed through this physical earth plane and on to spheres of light, they should have to return to the darkness of earth. There seems to them to be no reason, no logic in this; it refuses to fit in with their conception of an all-wise and all-loving Father–Mother God. Yet, dear ones, when the picture is more clearly drawn, we believe that you will face the future with much joy and hope.

Until you conceive clearly this wheel of rebirth, you will find most of the deeper problems of life obscure, you will fail to understand the justice of life. You will admit, because something within you compels you to admit it, that God is good, that God is an all-wise and all-loving Father and Mother. Yet there will remain problems beyond your solution. Nevertheless, you cling to the divine love, because the urge within you, which is divine, will direct you to the spirit of love.

The only way that you can touch the divine secrets of life is through the path of love and selflessness. Mind, which has its place in human evolution, can never of itself give the truth of the ancient wisdom, but it is necessary for the mind to be developed before a full comprehension of the universe can dawn. How does this touch the subject of reincarnation? Only because a great deal has been written concerning the sacred wisdom, and many seek to find truth through much reading. However, the heart of truth lies in the spirit, and only *you*, our beloved soul-brothers and sisters, can know truth; no-one else can give it to you. In the search for a clear understanding of reincarnation, we must become acquainted with the soul within. When we come face to face, we no longer cry for proof—the path of soul-evolution is known. This knowing is not something that you find in books.

The subject of reincarnation is a vast one, and we assure you that the crude idea of rebirth is a very inadequate description of what really takes place. Our first point is that the great universal questions can only be answered by gaining understanding of the process of the soul's evolution. Our second point is that life is growth; the purpose of life on physical earth is growth. And thirdly, this: human intelligence is confined by the finite mind, bound by time, and has no conception of the meaning of time. Humankind thinks threescore years and ten—or indeed a century—to be a very long period, when in truth it is only a flash. Little experience can be gained from one short period of earth life.

Now compare an ordinary person with a great soul, such as a master. Take the comparison between the two into your own self; examine well your soul. How many times have you fallen short of the ideal? It is true that all of us are human, but we are also divine, and the purpose of life is full development of the divine stature, or the Christ-being. The purpose of creation is that all the sons and daughters of God may develop into the fullness and glory of the Christ.

We can find no better symbol for incarnation than that of the seed planted in the darkness of earthly soil in order that it may grow into such fullness. The archetypal flower—the complete individual plant, too—is created first of all in the Divine Mind; and then the seed is planted in the earth to grow, to manifest. So with you, who are as a seed planted in physical form to grow towards the light until you become a child of God, perfect in life. You become the archetypal God-being, which God held in His–Her mind in the beginning. But if incarnation on the earth plane is so unimportant that you dwell there only for a symbolic seventy years, what a waste of creation! What a greenhouse for the divine shoot would be neglected, what a seed-bed would be left unsown!

Conceive the idea of the human soul, not as you know it—as the individual of everyday life—but as a soul that dwells in the heaven world. You all possess such a soul, and it relates to you as does a temple in the heavens compared with the tiny earthly abode that is your physical being. In the mystery schools of the past this idea was sometimes presented to the neophyte through masonry. Masonic imagery indeed offers a good illustration: the building of the temple. Each incarnation was identified with the rough ashlar, the stone that has its rough places and excrescences smoothed away so that it may be placed in the structure of the temple. In the building of the temple there can be nothing slipshod. There must be exactness, precision; an irregular block or square will throw the whole building out.

We would enlarge your conception of reincarnation, so that you put aside the idea of a small soul continually bobbing backwards and forwards. We want you to get the larger, grander idea of the continual growth of God-consciousness within this greater soul of yours.

## *Origins*

☙The concept of reincarnation is a part of what is known as the Ancient Wisdom. When we speak of the eternal things, we cannot touch any point and say, 'This is the beginning', because in the Ancient Wisdom there is no beginning. The wisdom of eternity has always been. It just *is*, like God the Creator. It is impossible for you to comprehend eternity with a finite mind. Only when you can escape the bounds of your personal self and touch the spheres that are called cosmic can you comprehend it. So while it is incorrect for us to say 'In the beginning', yet for you we must use these words in order to give a point from which you can work. At the same time, we would suggest that you endeavour in meditation to comprehend life as a circle.

This brings us to that ancient symbol of the circle with its central point, known to all astrologers as the symbol of the Sun. Always, there has been a centre of light, a central point of truth. From this central point all life has proceeded. Within all life as you know it on the physical plane is a centre that shines like a blazing sphere of light or a sun. The ancients worshipped that centre of life as God, knowing in their souls that that light was only visible to humankind as sunlight, but knowing that behind the sun was an even greater power and light. To this invisible light, invisible to mortal sight, they owed their very existence. Understand then with your heart, with your feeling, that behind the visible light of the sun is something else: a force, a power that holds you in a state of activity. You owe your life to that power. Everything in your world comes to you through that invisible power and it is the source of your spirit. This is what the ancients worshipped.

We would raise your consciousness to a life that every soul has once known in that Sun-sphere. From the Sun we all come. There is an answering echo in our innermost being when we speak of the Sun-sphere. All human beings sometimes make the mistake of thinking of the Sun- or the Christ-sphere as something towards which they are travelling. This is true, for it is a state of consciousness towards which they are moving; but you and we must all understand that it is a state of life from which we have all come. You still retain a power that enables you faintly to glimpse the glory of the Sun- or the Christ-sphere. It is only a vague hope, maybe, but each of you, because of your memories, can still understand that such a condition of life exists.

It would seem as though the soul has travelled far, far away, but has never lost the true consciousness of its source. Otherwise, it would not feel a yearning such as this, one to which even the most depraved soul can respond. True, it may be obscured and seemingly lost; but in times of dire need, in times of terrible grief and anguish, the soul will still reach out to its God, its Creator. The very yearning towards God is indicative of the life of God, or the universal Sun that dwells within each and every being.

At a time when we dwelt on earth long ago, the form of religion was Sun-worship. Sun-worship is still your religion, although it is not understood as it was in ages past. We have all worshipped the sun; we have all assembled in Solomon's temple. That is *Sol*omon's temple, the temple of the sun. This truth has lived in the heart of human beings right down the ages.

So, my brethren, let us meditate upon a state of life that is wholly in the light, in the heart of the glorious

Sun. Then within you the consciousness will grow that that is your true home, your source. However incomprehensible it may seem that your soul or spirit should have travelled so far, it is included in this divine plan that it should do so. It is because the soul takes on, or is clothed in, a body that it goes through all the trials and sorrows inherent in physical matter. That path is demonstrated in the life of Christ: in Jesus of Nazareth, the Son of God. It is the story of that perfect one in essence coming from the sphere of the sun, of the Christ, down, down, down into matter, and suffering torments of the physical plane. The life of Jesus Christ, which you can read about in the Bible, a life that was compressed into thirty-three years, is also symbolic of the life of every living soul. The thirty-three years of life represent the thirty-three degrees of initiation through which the soul passes on its journey, on its complete cycle from beginning to end.*

You see, brethren, it is only ignorance that prompts denial of the truth of reincarnation. The soul comes from the Sun-sphere; and when we speak of the Sun-sphere we are referring to the Great White Light, the eternal light in the heavens. God said, 'Let there be Light!' and there was light; and from that light everything was created. From that light we have all come;

---

*Similarly, and symbolically, there are thirty-three vertebrae in the human spine. This numbering of the initiations is probably not to be taken literally, although readers may like to follow up the subject in another 'White Eagle on…' book, INTUITION AND INITIATION.

to that light we all return, rich in experience and having gained wisdom, love and power. We attain at the end of that journey to the full stature of the human being—complete, perfect.

## The Brethren of the Sun

᠔Let us go far back to a time when there were, functioning behind the scenes of material life, groups of men and women formed in brotherhoods in many parts of the earth. These were known as brothers and sisters of the ancient cross within the circle. They were also known as brothers and sisters of the white cross—of the rosy cross, of the white cross, or of the star—and we also refer to them as the Illumined Ones. They function always in the same way, sending their influence, their knowledge, onto the outer plane of life to guide and inspire men and women about the true science and learning.

There are within the human soul two aspects, two types of vibration. There is the good, and there is what is called evil: the positive and the negative. Men and women have on occasion responded more to the negative or the dark forces than to the good forces. Those behind the scenes work untiringly to hold a sufficient balance to keep the world steady on its course. The lesson of equilibrium has to be learned by the soul. The importance, then, of your own response to the positive or the light vibrations is very great, particularly today, because the world has reached a critical stage in its evolution. This is why a greater effort than ever is being made by the Illumined Ones, the brethren of the white light, to help humankind.

We told you earlier that, alive ourselves in those days, we worshipped the Sun. You might say that ours was worship of the source of all being. That worship of the Sun has come down through the ages as a religion of many peoples. As we have already said, many different names are given to the one central truth, and there are many paths that lead back to the same central truth. However, the first principle is exactly the same, whichever path the soul takes—the first principle of response to the vibrations of the white light and the subsequent control or balance of those vibrations that are called negative. These are what you are building into your soul today, and at this very moment. They are creating your karma in your next life and the next life and so on. You are either rising up in the scale or you are deteriorating. If it is the latter, when the time comes for you to rise again you will not find it so easy. This has happened many times to many souls.

You count time by the path of the Sun and the hours, days, weeks, years, and so on; but you have no conception at all of the nature of time. When you get into the realms of spirit, time does not exist because life is consciousness, not measured in time. When you think of your everyday life, you think of the one incarnation; and when you review it you have cause for serious thought. How far have you progressed spiritually, you ask yourself?

This you do not know. When you are able to see back, to touch that higher soul-consciousness, you will see how many, many times you have returned to the earth, and what a long time it has taken for your soul to gain sufficient powers to control your emotions and your mental flights—to say nothing of your physical habits! Again and again, the soul returns to work out its karma, to pay off its debts. Sometimes it slips back, sometimes it moves a little way forward, but it is a long journey.

Now you will cry, 'What a terrible prospect, White Eagle!'. No, not at all, because everything in this present as well as in future incarnations depends upon your effort to respond to the white light within life, to the influence of the brethren behind the veil, to the impetus for good. It is possible for a soul so to work towards the light in one incarnation that it passes through the portals of initiation into the state of freedom or liberation from rebirth.

Be sure that life goes on and on. Sometimes it is a question of withdrawing for a period for a rest and for refreshment in the world of spirit. Then, at the appointed time, you feel ready to proceed again.

There are many souls who have passed beyond the need for reincarnation, having freed themselves from the bondage of the physical life. Throughout the ages there have been wise men and women (sometimes called God-beings) who have been sent to your earth planet as divine witnesses. Many of these great ones or masters have traversed the lower levels of life until they have reached freedom. They live now in a higher ether, but have power over physical matter. They are brothers and sisters of the Great White Light, which means the universal lodge or home of all perfected souls. All of them have had many incarnations on earth. All share certain qualities, certain characteristics; above all, they have all risen to the level of sustained God thought: living in God, for God, and to serve God's creation. They manifest at all times the one supreme Law of Love.

Now all these great Ones when in incarnation have the same Spirit of Christ, the same Divine Light, shining through their human personality. At different ages, according to the state of evolution of human consciousness, these teachers have come. Their message appears to have different meanings until it is analyzed and contemplated from an esoteric aspect. Always, however, the main message has been to bid the soul to seek the Light, to seek God. Some have gone so far as to say, 'I am the Light' and that the 'I am' is the Light. *Before Abraham was, I am*—this is the First Great Cause. It is impossible for your finite minds to comprehend infinity, to comprehend eternity. Why should you? You are very small as yet, but you must live in belief, in faith in that supreme Light. And why? Because, when you come to examine life as a whole you will find that that

Light controls all life. It is itself the First Great Cause of all things. This can prove itself to you in your daily life and also in the whole plan of your life, if you will obey life's commands, if you will obey life's law.

## Links of Old

ॐAs students of our words, you are part of a company of brethren who are all seeking the light of the spirit, and you are aided by those illumined brethren who come back to help you in your search. They are the hidden companions of your journey. They know you, although you may not know them in your physical consciousness. They are the companions whom you meet when you enter into a state of meditation, when you are withdrawn from the world, or when you leave your physical body at the time of sleep. Later on at death you will meet these beloved ones, for they are your true companions and the spiritual life is your real life. You have stepped down from a land of light into darkness. You have donned something like a diver's suit for this purpose, descending into the depths to search for treasure, for the pearl of great price. It is wise to get a truer perspective of life, unwise to think of mortal life as all-important, although it has its significance, of course.

Each time we speak to you, we have to remind you of the company of shining angelic ones who are with us. We do this because we understand the heaviness of the flesh and earthly mind. Some people living forget or do not know that they have many unseen friends, relatives and companions. They naturally think of people about them as being the only ones who know them, the only people whom they know. They forget—indeed they do not know—that they have lived through many, many ages and in the course of their long journey through matter they have met, lived with, and enjoyed the friendship of many, many souls. So bear this in mind: that you have around you beloved companions, some of whom you know, and a number you do not. In the course of your spiritual unfoldment you will hold communion with these friends unseen.

This should be a source of comfort to those of you who feel lonely, particularly those who live in a family that cannot share your interests. If you are in such condition, remember you are there by your own choice and for a purpose; and that you have in spirit your true family, who are people in perfect harmony with your spirit, and who help you to live your life nobly, wisely, profitably. These invisible brethren are souls with whom you have lived in past incarnations and with whom you have a great bond of sympathy and love. It is also true that in your present life you are sometimes brought into contact with people with whom you instantly feel at home. Then you know instinctively that they too are very old friends or former relatives. Beyond these, there are souls with whom you are brought into close and intimate relationship, yet with whom you feel you have nothing in common—yet you know that there must be a link of some kind. Therefore think of yourself as having a very large company of friends moving along the path of life with you. However alone you may appear, yet you are not alone. Quite the reverse!

# Chapter Two

## *Knowing we have Lived Before*

THERE ARE some who know intuitively that they have lived before. They see life not as the cramped, finite one they are now living, but as a long, long journey full of interest, full of experiences which have brought them happiness; which have brought them richness, knowledge, understanding. They know that reincarnation is a truth. Why do some people know this and others appear to be quite shut away from such a realization? We suggest it is because the former have earned the right by their karma to become aware, to realize in this incarnation. Yet there are others who appear to have their consciousness limited to this life alone because they have not reached the point where the eternity of life reveals itself.

There is another old question which many ask, 'Why is it we cannot remember our past lives?' We would point out that this is because memory of their past does not rest with their physical memory of the present. The impressions, the memories of the past, are stored in the celestial home, the celestial self. Unless the soul has earned the right to tap into that celestial temple or self it cannot remember. Such memory is not in the physical brain. Unless the soul has developed sufficiently to unlock the secrets of the celestial self then it cannot remember.

The reaction of the material thinker towards the subject of reincarnation has been the same. 'Why cannot we remember our past lives?'. But if you pause to think of the difficulty with which the adult remembers details of his or her childhood, or even details of life a few years ago, you will readily recognize how hard it would be to recall happenings of even a century, and perhaps of many thousands of years ago, with the physical brain. This same brain has never received the impress of happenings of past lives. Such memories are stored not in the brain but in your soul.

In order to open up a clear picture of the past, it is necessary through meditation and inward contemplation to touch the soul-vibrations. Something of this picture has impressed itself upon your feelings, and although possibly not very defined, it may be very true. You may 'feel' that you once lived, say, in Egypt or in ancient Greece. These countries seem familiar to you. People will say, 'Oh, but this may so easily be due to imagination'. We will not stop on this occasion to define imagination, but we will say this—that such feelings about places and people are likely to be correct. Take care, though: it is not what you think, not what you would like to be, but what you feel within your soul is what has actually been.

As you proceed on the path of this inner unfoldment, you will become more sensitive to the vibrations of the past experiences stored away in your soul. Those vibrations create in your mind pictures of your past. In the halls of learning in the spirit world, it is the usual procedure to throw upon an etheric screen scenes of past events culled either from the life of some particular pupil or—should it be for a class or group—from the world's history. These scenes are unremembered on earth except by those who have an inner knowledge. Records such as these are ones which are left impressed on the ethers of the earth.

We hope that we have been able to give you a clear picture of what we mean by the akashic records, as they are called. Only when the soul has awakened is it able to read them. There may be many deficiencies in your records on stone or parchment, but no deficiency exists in the akashic records.

It is possible for the higher consciousness to know the form its previous incarnations have taken. But you won't get at your previous incarnations by searching with the mind. When through development and growth of the higher consciousness you are ready for the door to be opened, you will get flashes of light perhaps coming through with intervals of many years. When you have had these flashes, no amount of argument will ever shake your belief. Flashes of memory from past lives come very often in the early morning after sleep, because in sleep the soul is often in contact with that larger consciousness.

## *There are no Rules about when you Return*

☙You may ask, how long it is between each incarnation? Bear this in mind: we cannot lay down a hard and fast rule. We cannot say that you reincarnate every two hundred years—it would be wrong. If we tell you that a person passes out of one body into another immediately, we should be wrong again. If we say to you that there may be thousands of years between each incarnation, we would still not be correct. In every case it depends upon the individual. But it is possible for a soul to reincarnate quickly for a special purpose.

The soul is in search of experience. When it reincarnates, it may be drawn many times to the same country. It may be drawn to the vicinity of its former life if its karma lies there, if it is there that its opportunity waits to gain the knowledge it seeks. As an example, for ages past the soul incarnating in the East has had an opportunity to absorb wisdom. For centuries the soul incarnating in the West has had a different opportunity, that of putting into action the wisdom it once absorbed in the East.

It is not only its own self that the soul has to think about. It is all the other selves, the soul's companions over a series of lives. It realizes that humanity is part of itself. It feels compassion and love for all humankind. Through this love comes the urge to help humanity to rise. So it is *love* that urges the soul back, love for God

and love for humankind. While power of a certain
kind is the urge that causes the descent of the race,
love brings about the human reascent to the divine
Father–Mother, God. All the debts made in life are
the debts of power—which you call evil; or the debts
of love—which you call good.

We remind you again that continents that seem to
have vanished from the face of the earth still exist on
the etheric planes, and that what you think of as lives
you once lived are not past lives at all. They are still
ever-present, as many of you can testify. For you can
go back and instantly re-live any life or part of any life
of your past, because past and present are all bound
up together and inseparable. Their impressions are all
there in the ether and can be tapped and seen at any
moment in your meditations.

You are, even now, within the whole of life. It is
your consciousness that has to develop and expand,
so that you realize you are not confined to one little
tiny space on the earth plane, but are in infinity. You
are within the centre of the circle: the heart of all life.
You are in infinity … you are *it* … you are with God.
It is only a question of your own consciousness, your
own belief, your inner knowing that you are in God.
When you know that you are in God, that all is of
God, that God is all around you and within you, then
you can get some idea of what we mean when we say
there is no time, no space. Time is in the eternal now.
When you can overcome the idea of time and space

and limitation, and when you have realized that true and perfect Christ love, which is ever-present with you; when you have realized in yourself those things—infinity, eternity and love—then you will never die. The realization of this takes many, many incarnations to grow: however, that is the goal of life.

Seek therefore to tune in, to adjust yourself to that great life, the life that is your life. For you have lived through countless ages—some lives happy and some the reverse—but you have been learning all the time, and the little light of divinity within you is growing. As this light grows within you, you become more like a true son or daughter of the living God.

## *Power and Love*

&Your Bible tells you that God has given to you the birthright of free will. Your world at present is beginning to respond to this. For many centuries, human beings have been in subjection, but now they are beginning to exert choice. The human race has been in search of power for many centuries, and so has become at times dominated by and overwhelmed by power; it has created what you understand as karma. Each time a soul has reincarnated it has to meet its karmic debts, to suffer pain and to experience joy. Pain is the result of desire for domination over a thing; joy and happiness are the result of a soul allowing the light of love to rule all its actions.

It seems, then, that these two aspects—power and love—are the two teachers of the soul. Ultimately, there will have to come a reconciliation and absorption of these two aspects so that power and love become blended and at one, an absorption of darkness into the light. This will mean a restoration of equilibrium in the world. At present power is the dominant factor, but the time will come when the two factors are balanced.

Although the tiny spark of divine life is perfect, it is impossible for most humans to be born with the full consciousness of God developed. The God-consciousness lies very deeply buried. Look at a little brown seed and you can hardly realize that if that seed is planted it can grow into a plant bearing beautiful blooms. This wonderful miracle is wrought not by a human gardener but by something you cannot comprehend. The point is that within that seed itself lies the potential to grow.

This is an illustration of the divine life in every human being. The seed leaves the divine Father–Mother; it is planted in earth exactly as a seed is planted. When you begin to think of the beauty, the majesty, the radiance, the unimaginable glory of God, you know that that seed cannot attain to God in one short life. Think of the average person you know, however good he or she appears. What new growth is there in a person in one life? Not a great deal, in the majority of cases. Thinking like this will give you some idea how long it takes for that spark of divine life to mature into an image of its Creator. Only through the soul living in physical matter can it be so disciplined as to bring forth the glory of God in the soul.

We have spoken of two attributes of the Godhead: love and power. These two grand tests come before the individual spirit repeatedly, in every incarnation. Either the soul desires power with which to dominate others, or it responds to the light of love. When the soul chooses power it is sinking into the depths. When it follows the path of love it is rising into the heights. These are the two great urges. When the path of love is chosen, love attains not the power of domination but of blessing.

The initiate who may be called a White Brother is one who has attained power through love. On the other hand, the souls who have attained only power for power's sake are clothed in dark raiment. Many there are who through more than one incarnation—through many incarnations sometimes—have sought for power and have used that power to gain domination over others in a magical way. This is called black magic. It carries with it heavy karma. Some are today working out karma created by them in past lives and on continents which are now extinct physically but which still remain in the ether. It was the power complex that caused the destruction of countless numbers of physical lives when a cataclysm overtook the earth and its very surface was changed.

The souls who pass out of the physical reincarnate again, again, and again to work out the karma they have made. Thereby the spirit learns through experience the right way to power, the meaning of power, even as it learns the beauty and wisdom of love. This is the reason for reincarnation. Time is impossible to measure. You are confused when we say that time does not exist. You measure time perhaps by the Sun or some instrument, but we repeat that when you have escaped from this finite life you will realize that there is no measuring of time in spirit.

An occultist will tell you of certain continents which were in existence which have now disappeared; but the face of the earth today is entirely changed from what it was some millions of years ago. Streams of human life have come and gone; people have lived and reincarnated again and again and again and have finally passed away. Other streams have come, other cycles of life, and they too have passed beyond this physical plane. It is impossible to estimate the number of lives that the individual soul lives on earth and not easy to assess how far distant those lives are from each other.

Sometimes the soul will spend a long period resting in the heaven world. Then it appears that when the spiritual evolution of a race is reaching its climax there is a much quicker reincarnation of its souls. This may be particularly true of the more evolved, who may be eager to come back and get on with the work of helping others up from the depths of darkness and suffering.

It is known that a child will return quickly if that soul is eager to make progress.

When the soul, freed from the physical body, regains its heavenly home it has the 'vision glorious' of its Creator. Then it has only one desire—to become Godlike. The knowledge is borne upon that soul that there is only one way of becoming Godlike, and that the way is one of self-discipline. The only way for the soul to acquire self-discipline is to take upon itself the clothing of physical matter, because only in physical matter does discipline come to the soul. When it realizes this truth—as it does again and again—then it is ready to dive back into matter to work, to strive, to become more perfect.

All the qualities of God are inherent in the soul while it is as a babe, but they have to grow, and during growth have to be tested. Many times the spirit is overwhelmed by the conditions in which it finds itself, and it creates for itself karma. This karma causes reincarnation. Thus it is the least evolved aspect of the soul that is drawn back to the earth to reincarnate. The soul in the heaven world sends out projections, and it is these that come into incarnation. The whole of the individual self is not usually in incarnation; this happens at most occasionally, even rarely. The higher aspect, the greater self, remains in the heaven world. When the incarnate soul can sufficiently open its consciousness to make contact with its true or its greater self, the flood of light comes through and raises that little self to the greater. You say, 'What is the good of trying to be any better? What is the use of anything?'. This is the answer, we tell you: that the aspiration, the urge to be good on the part of the little self, will raise it and bring close communion and close contact with that greater, more glorious self in the heavens.

# Chapter Three

## *In God's Image*

WE HAVE referred to the need for incarnation, and seen the individual life as a seed of great promise. We have seen the soul as beautiful, with Godlike potentialities. Before we proceed with this theme, let us make clear our meaning. Every human being is created in God's image. Each one of us is the thought of God. You are a perfect child of God. The thought of perfection is a good thought to hold to as you journey through the world, when the soul is building a temple for the habitation of the perfect son–daughter of God: all-good, all-wisdom, all-love, all-truth. The evolution of the soul means no more or less than the building of this temple.

To emphasize this, let us change our image: spirit itself is the perfect jewel. The soul is its setting, or the casket which contains the jewel. The work of the soul is to allow that perfect jewel of divine spirit to manifest in glory, both through the soul and eventually through physical matter. The jewel shines and manifests perfection through the personality or physical nature. The sole purpose of reincarnation is for this eventual manifestation. Through the plan of evolution, you manifest perfection and happiness. God created you for happiness. God created beauty for you. God gave to every son–daughter an inner light to guide him or her on the journey.

What you have to understand is that through earthly experience the soul is being continually built of material that has been earned on earth. All human beings are builders. All will some day be master masons. Joy and happiness come through understanding.

It is impossible for the physical mind to comprehend the infinite plan of life. All you can do is to endeavour to keep your vision upon the one grand truth that God is light, that you—the divine spirit—are also light. The six-pointed Star is a symbol of the perfect manifestation of spirit in matter.

There are many paths of life on earth and in other spheres. God did not create His–Her sons and daughters to suffer, but to enjoy the gifts of love; and this lies behind the whole purpose of life and reincarnation. From your limited experience, you know that you have to earn knowledge, to earn the exquisite sensations of joy and love. Those of you who have passed through great tribulations can look back upon the episode with thankfulness, realizing that you have extracted from them a sweetness and beauty of the spirit. This alone gives you happiness. It is sometimes difficult to look forward with anticipation, but it is easier to look back with thankfulness.

To use your words to convey spiritual truth is difficult, because they are so clumsy. Maybe that is why silence is the rule in the lodge above. Truth is an inward knowing, an awareness of God and the divine plan.

You will come to understand that when a person has reached a certain stage, he or she inwardly recognizes both the mortal self and the Christ self. You yourself play in one sense the part of a spectator, but you are also a participant because you find yourself drawn sometimes to the one and sometimes to the other. You may ask, 'What is that essential part which is the spectator and yet the participant—the innermost *I* which knows these things?'.

The essential self that looks upon the drama is the jewel, the pure spirit. It looks upon the work that is building the soul. Into the building of the temple goes the material, the substance of both aspects of life. We struggle to describe this duality because most of you find it difficult to comprehend the blending of black and white, good and evil. Some say evil is very real; others say evil does not exist except in good. Evil and good are one and the same thing. These two aspects of being—the sorrowful one and the happy one—are one and the same. You think they are separate, but they are not. This is a truth difficult to understand. These two aspects are the material that the jewel or the divine spark is using to build the perfect temple or soul.

Also, there are other states of life to which the soul can go. The earth is not the only world upon which life exists. When the soul is attached to the earth, this usually goes on until it has achieved the object of its creation on the earth. Until a certain condition of God-consciousness is reached, there is only one school for the soul—the earth. When it has earned its degrees it can pass into the university—or on to another planet.

## *Body, Soul and Spirit*

&When we come to you from the world of spirit, our endeavour is to raise your consciousness beyond the earthly mind so that you can absorb heavenly truth. The mind has to be developed to a very fine degree before it can comprehend such truth. The average man and woman has not yet reached this stage. This is the reason they cannot comprehend. In the process of reincarnation, that higher mind is being evolved, unfolded, but the process is slow—exceedingly slow in some cases.

We have tried to convey to you in language the pathway the soul travels. We may have repeated ourselves, and purposely, because what is said is so often lost. Again and again it must be repeated until at last the soul absorbs and understands the spiritual meaning behind the words employed. Until the higher mind is ready, it is impossible for anyone to understand fully the eternal verities, but experiences through life after life cause this development of a vehicle that will enable the soul while it is still embodied to understand and to see truth as it was from the beginning—shall we say from the centre of the circle of life?

We should like to move on now to tell you about the varying degrees of consciousness. Let us commence by helping you to understand what is meant by the word 'soul'; for if you can clearly conceive the soul as distinct from the mind and the spirit, you perhaps will be able to understand the varying degrees of consciousness which we all experience. So many different labels are used to describe the different aspects of the being. Most of you are aware of possessing more than the physical body, and that the physical body is merely the channel for manifestation on the physical plane, through which the soul works to gain experience, to absorb consciousness. You have a physical body, a soul body, and the light within. The divine urge, the light within ... this is the light which is the very life of God and is the determining factor in your birth. You come to birth through that light of the spirit directing your soul, directing the ship as it sets forth on its voyage of discovery. The experiences gained by the soul during its journey through life are the materials that go to build the soul and become the very fabric of which the soul is built. That which is not wanted is consumed and that which passes the test is built into the soul temple.

Keep in mind the vision of that larger self, of that greater consciousness in the celestial planes, and think of an incarnation as a feeler, sent forth from the higher consciousness into matter. It descends to pass through earth-experiences, to gather certain materials that the soul needs to make it perfect. You all possess that larger consciousness, and in the present day of life it may be a part of you that is manifesting, one which has not manifested before.

Let us show you a wider view, a grander panorama of the great truth of reincarnation. The soul does not enter the body fully at physical birth, but gradually as the years advance. At about the physical age of twenty-one, the full incarnating soul has generally arrived. However, the contact of the soul with the physical body is made before physical conception. The soul is born into the physical body with a certain quality of consciousness, and this quality exerts a determining factor on the physical body—that is to say, on the nervous system, the bloodstream and the glands. Thus your present life will determine the quality of your soul not only for later years, but for the life to follow on the astral and higher planes of spiritual life; and, following these, the nature and quality of your next incarnation. You may thus recognize the importance of your contacts in normal and everyday life!

The physical bodies into which you are born, the etheric bodies which make the bridge between the world of matter and the world of spirit, the mental bodies by which you understand the laws of life and gain experience of the earth life—all these vehicles are the result of the past. Today you are creating or building the atoms into your soul that will be used to form future vehicles through which you will manifest, if not on the planet earth, then possibly on another planet of this earth's system. Therefore, upon you rests the choice. You may build into your soul disease-atoms through neglect and wilfulness, and particularly through neglecting opportunities to learn of the inner wisdom; you may limit yourself by your own free will. The Lords of Karma can only rebuild bodies with the material you offer them.

## *Falling and Rising Again*

❧The human was born onto this earth plane not as a microbe and not, as other people think, as the smallest cell! The physical evolved from the cell, but not the spirit of humankind, and not the form of the human as you know it. Humankind was created by God in God's own image and was given the key to heaven, although the mind and intellect were not as developed as now. At its creation humanity received the basis or foundation of a religion: one which is so simple. It is a religion of love and brotherhood, a religion of service to all aspects of life.

Some people believe that the divine spark within has evolved from a very low estate, up through the various kingdoms of life. That is true in one sense and yet incorrect in another: there is an apparent contradiction. We mean by this that the divine spark or life was

breathed into the form of man–woman in the beginning. God created perfect creatures in outward form
and breathed into these perfect creatures the God-life.
God thereby gave to each man or woman—to each
being—a perfect form. This gift of Spirit gave to each
being the power of freewill choice.

In the beginning, life was beautiful. However, because men and women possessed this power of choice
they desired to experiment just as a child desires to play
with a new toy. As soon as a child feels its feet it wants
to walk! As soon as it knows that it can produce sound
it wants to talk. This applies to the soul as well as the
body. The soul, feeling power and knowledge, wants to
experiment; and in the process it makes mistakes. As it
makes mistakes it creates karma. Karma is the teacher
of the soul. Thereafter, it has to go through countless
lives and countless experiences, learning from its own
karma and thus learning the wisdom and the love of
the Perfect One.

Humanity is created perfect in form, but as a babe
in understanding. It can only grow in understanding
through experience, through trial and error. This process goes on through aeons and aeons of time. Indeed
when you think of God, your Creator, the Great Light
in the heavens, and compare your own insignificance
with that magnificence, you will begin to understand
why you have to travel such a long journey back to that
Source of Life.

We would have you regard the fall of humankind

as a process of evolution, and not a violation of the divine plan of progress. A beautiful babe is both sweet and innocent, but if a person continued to be a beautiful baby all through life on earth he or she would be of little ultimate use. God created souls pure and good, but they had no sense—to put it crudely! They had to learn through reason to attain to wisdom, and had to walk the path of evolution and growth. So they descended through the various planes and then had to re-ascend, so that they could become as God, with the power to create. Procreation, reproduction of the human body was the first step; but man–woman has to learn more. He–she has to learn the creative secret of the universe.

Witness the coming of the serpent—indicative of wisdom—which we would tell you came to enlighten men and women and not to tempt them. Imagine the first Light Bearer saying to the new creation, 'You have the power within yourselves to create life!'. Before, men and women had no power, they were entirely dependent upon the angelic ones. Now, they have to be responsible. 'You have bodies, you can create—what does it matter if you die? More bodies can be created from yours.' Cannot you see subtly the idea of sin entering in with this, bringing to humankind suffering, sickness, pain and death?

The young soul of humanity had to grow, and the only way for it to learn was by descent into the very depths of the physical, by life akin to the animal, with all the very deepest, strongest passions working in it. Consider also not only the physical, but the invisible forces of, shall we say, 'the devil' at work on the soul, which had the effect of drawing it into the very depths of 'sin' or 'self'. Before the soul can become unselfed or God-conscious, it must have developed full self. When humanity lay in that lowest state of self, it could only be turned back again through love—love being the antithesis of self. Therefore we say that only through the love principle can humanity be redeemed or saved from destruction through self.

On this upward path, these physical bodies that you know now will change. Your bodies today are different from those of the last root race, for there has been a process of purification and rarefication of the physical. It will continue until at last humankind will not know death, but only a transmutation, even as was demonstrated by Jesus the Christ.


## Continual Growth of God-Consciousness

ᐒWe are trying to show you that you possess a soul in the heaven world and that it is like a circle that surrounds the spirit. The spirit directs the path of life; therefore, we say God directs the path of life. God is the urge; God urges you to the highest, even sometimes against the will of the lower mind, the lower self, or self-will. As spirit or divine spark, God directs the life of

the soul, choosing its way through many incarnations
or experiences of earthly life. Each time a part of that
soul descends, it absorbs certain forms of experience
necessary for the growth and evolution of the greater
soul above.

Sometimes in your experience you receive a flash
from the higher self, and even recognize such in
individuals who apparently are quite undeveloped.
Never make the mistake, beloved children, of judging
anyone. Never look at a soul and say, 'Poor thing, it
is unevolved', for you know nothing of what you say;
and it may be that the one who appears degraded is a
soul of purity and great beauty in the heaven world.
Appearances are always deceptive.

When a soul has evolved, it is shown several paths
from which it may choose. One such path is reincarnation, but a soul may choose a different form of service—perhaps as a guide and helper. Possibly a third
path will be the opportunity to work with the angels.
But reincarnation is often chosen by the evolving soul.
Do not run away with the idea that to reincarnate is
to retrogress. Reincarnation is spiritual evolution, because each time you re-enter physical life you become
more beautiful. There are souls freed from the wheel
of rebirth who return voluntarily in order to help
humanity.

Reincarnation means just this, that the human
soul, the divine spark sent forth from God, comes into
incarnation on the physical plane until it has become

God-conscious. Once that awareness is fully awakened, the soul need not incarnate again.

# Chapter Four

## *Creating the Temple of Light:*
## *the Celestial Body*

ALL LIFE is governed by divine law. People sometimes object to the idea of reincarnation, and say that
nothing will induce them to come back to earth. But
this will not affect the outworking of the law, for the
time will come when they will naturally want to come
back—because they will see from a higher state of
life the desirability of returning to the labours of the
earthly life. In Freemasonry it is said that the soul goes
from labour to refreshment, and from refreshment to
labour—from labour on earth to refreshment in the
heavens, we would say. This, the law of reincarnation
expressed in simple terms, is a cosmic law that cannot
be disobeyed.

When you pass out of the physical body, you enter
a state corresponding to what our Roman Catholic
friends describe as 'purgatory', but one we would
describe as just a waiting place. It is a state the soul
has prepared for itself during its earth sojourn, by
the quality of its life. We would like you to get a very
true picture of this state. For the young soul, it can be
coarse and crude, because the soul knows no better;

with the ordinary person, it can be a very pleasant life with gardens, fair landscapes, pleasant homes. All the material has been gathered for the building of these homes during the person's life on earth. Unconsciously, you prepare for yourself the kind of place you will be in when you leave your physical body.

Is it not beautiful and comforting to know that a heavenly garden for rest and refreshment and communion with your loved ones awaits you after the long 'day' on earth? Try to use your imagination. Don't allow yourselves to be so tightly screwed down to earth. Imagine what it could be like to enter that heavenly garden and meet again friends whom you thought you had lost. It's a lovely thought, isn't it? But we assure you it is a more lovely thing to experience.

At a certain level, above the mental plane, there is built what we call the 'Temple of Light'. It is at a high level of life. From that level the soul returns to incarnation, but it can dwell there in a state of supreme happiness and bliss, enjoying all the beauties of a lovely world and a lovely life for a long, long time, after its strenuous life of service on earth. There is no hard and fast rule. There is no forcing the soul into reincarnation, although it is the law of life to return some time. At a certain state of its spiritual evolution the soul quickens—awakens, as it were. It quickens in consciousness and desires to come back to retrace its steps and reincarnate, not only to gain more knowledge but often to give wider and greater service. In this process of growth, remember that myriad souls have been born into physical life. They have incarnated many times, and in many, many cases have passed through the entire university of earthly life onward to other spheres. We are trying to convey in simple words and by simple pictures the immensity and intricacy of life. You look out into your world of today and perhaps feel terrified by what you see. You think in terms of tragedy when things go wrong. Yet we would have you hold a better, higher and deeper conception of the process of human development—of growth, of spiritual evolution—and keep your vision ever upon the golden world, the golden age that will come.

This must dawn, we assure you, as it has already come in the past. You will now wonder, if the golden age once existed on the earth, why humanity has lost it? Well, you see, it all comes into the picture of night following day, of in-breathing and out-breathing—of the slow but gradual perfecting of life, not necessarily as you understand perfection but as it is understood at a higher level. When you can comprehend the glory of God's creation, you will then see the purpose of this rhythm, this 'in and out'. Let us give you the analogy of birth and death, of successive reincarnations. When you come into a body, you come as to a school wearing an earthly body. Your soul is breathed in by the breath of the Great White Spirit, and later breathed out again into the illimitable beauty of higher worlds. After a period of rest and refreshment, you are breathed in again.

This is the rhythm of life; you come into reincarnation and then drop the physical body; but you continue, the essential you continues still.

When the incarnating soul passes from the physical body, it goes through the astral plane, passes onwards through the mental planes, and arrives eventually in what you call the heaven world, or a condition of the higher consciousness or 'temple', just as we have described. Then the soul is merged. It becomes at one with God; it slips into the ocean of God-consciousness. As a drop slips into the ocean, so it can always be withdrawn from the ocean—there is no such thing as separation, and yet all atoms are separate. When the soul is in that state, is so glorified, it is able to see what is needed—and so another journey is made—and so a part of the soul is sent forth again to bring back yet more material for the temple. So you will see that after a soul has passed through various incarnations, in one sense it merges into the one great whole, and need not incarnate again. Up to that point, reincarnation is necessary, because the soul, being as a babe, or a very young child, is incapable of using its will and selecting for itself the wisest or the best path.

## No Force

‍We do not wish to enforce our opinion on anyone, but reincarnation, like life and death, is a law, and whether you believe it or not makes no difference. But we do recognize that you have free will and are not withdrawn from heaven and cast back into fleshly life willy-nilly. So long as a soul declares, 'I do not want to go back to earth', the answer comes, 'Well, my child, rest, there is no hurry … no hurry'. God does not hurry.

You may say to us, 'But, White Eagle, I cannot come back again to earth and all its suffering—once is quite enough!'. We, too, might be ones to query it. 'Why should we come back into the fog and mists and darkness of the earth plane when we might remain in heaven?' We know how beautiful is heaven, and we want to tell you, to try to help you in your daily life to solve your difficulties. We can see perhaps a little clearer than you, and may be able to help. Because of this we come; because of this it is a joy to come; and unless we come we can find no peace in heaven, because we cannot enjoy peace knowing that humanity is suffering and needing the little help and the balm our presence might bring.

You won't come back so long as you think 'I don't want to'. When you decide to be reborn, you have reached that sphere where the light illumines you and you know the purpose of life. You have seen yourself, a little, unfinished, poor and miserable mortal; for you compare yourself as you are to the glories you see in the celestial plane. You cry 'My Father–Mother, I long to be as Thee!'. 'How can I attain? How can I best serve

Thee? For I love thee, O God!'. And the answer is, 'Child, you must work to become perfected; you must live and you must toil on earth'. 'O Father–Mother, then I go, send me forth! I go ... I go to perfect myself.' The soul no longer shrinks, but longs for the experience.

We are asked, 'What of my miserable little consciousness here, White Eagle? I know nothing of this glory'. No, maybe not. But there is a voice within which knows all things ... the voice of the silence. 'Be still ... and know God.' Keep this brain still ... be quiet, and God shall speak, for the voice of the silence knows, and the voice ever says to you, 'Onward, onward ... love, kindness, humility, tolerance, charity'. Intellect does not say this. Mind says, 'Each one for himself or herself in this world'. But the voice whispers again, 'Meekness ... peace ... love'. Even so do we hear, coming down the ages, in the same gentle voice, *Love one another.*

In the case of young souls, the choice is not so much given to the individual, in the beginning, as to the group soul.\* The group soul will direct the good of the group. The younger souls incarnate more in the sense of groups; they find themselves in certain conditions, which in the beginning are difficult. That is not saying that all in poverty, for example, are young souls. There may be those who have chosen that condition.

The soul unawakened to spiritual truth is caught up in the rhythm of life and passes through various lives

\*The concept of the group soul is explained further on pages 75–9.

and cycles of life until it attains a state of consciousness where God says, 'Now you have attained just so much. You can see your path; your guide will be near you, watching your steps and ready to help but will not interfere with your will. Your will is yours for the purpose of enabling the consciousness of God to grow and function within you. And so you may use your will and choose your path'.

All is a question of evolution. When you have reached that understanding where you can choose and decide for yourself, you will so long to get back into harness that the question will be, 'How soon can I go?'.

You would not be reading this book if in some previous life you had not responded to some karmic lesson and in doing so received a minor, or perhaps a major, initiation. At all events, in a previous life an expansion of consciousness came to you, an experience clearly shown when you passed out of the earth body, and journeyed to the spheres above. You were then given an opportunity. You were shown by your teacher, or by one of the elder wise ones, possible channels, or possible lives on earth. 'You may choose this one, or this one or this one—any one of these lives will enable you, if you are diligent, to attain that degree of consciousness which you now desire.' Your soul, in those high places, was shown the prize, and that only through certain experiences on earth could you gain that knowledge so sorely needed, and for which you were thirsting. A choice of lives was revealed to you, and you were shown what each life offered. You, your deepest understanding, decided into which life and which family you would be born.

At the same moment you were also given the opportunities of the lesser or the greater degree. Your soul chose either to hurry, or to take things in leisurely fashion. Therefore now, if a big piece of karma comes, say, 'I chose that; I am going to get on with it!'. We repeat that there is really no forcing, because the soul has its choice. So long as you go on saying, 'Nothing will induce me to come back!', you won't come back; but when you see something very lovely, and learn that it will not be yours until you go back to earth, eventually you will say, 'Yes; I must have that beautiful thing'. The higher self sees; but the lower self kicks very hard and rebels. Yet the higher self is inspiring and urging it forward all the time. It may be that the soul does not gain what it longs for in one incarnation, but will eventually. It is better not to rebel!

We hope we have reassured you that the soul comes back to the earth (although people will not believe this) of its own free will, in order to gain certain lessons, or to give certain service. When clothed in the lower sheaths of existence, and lastly in the physical body, the higher or God-consciousness is so covered that you cannot believe that you chose your life. You may say, 'Nonsense! I certainly did not choose this'. No! Your lower self did not choose, not the rebellious self—that certainly did not. But the pure God-consciousness, the higher part of your being, chose it, because it knew that only by travelling through that particular scenery of life would you gain the quality of consciousness for which you sought.

You are reading this because at some time you have seen the vision of what lay before you. Your consciousness has expanded. In this day of life, in this incarnation, you have been guided and urged by that higher self to seek contact with spiritual truth, with the inner and occult truths. You are therefore drawn to places, or seek certain books and contacts. Sometimes the contacts are brought to you, opportunities come; sometimes you absorb the truth, and sometimes not. But even trifles have their place: every thing in your life has its place, its purpose, and is destined to bring to you, consciously or unconsciously, further evolution and light.

## A Matter of Vibration

❧From what we have previously said, you will have learned that in earth life each individual builds into its soul what we call vibrations. They are are the result of its life in matter, and the soul is full of such vibrations. When a child is born, it brings into incarnation the sum total of its experiences as a structure it has built in the past. In this structure, which is called the soul, there are countless millions of these vibrations resonating in the human life. Thus the soul from its birth is subject to desires: it is stimulated to thought, word and action. The desires urge the individual to positive or negative thoughts and actions, or what are called good or evil. These two impulses apply in everyone. This should cause you to think seriously about your thoughts and actions, because everything which is thought, said, and done is not transient, but built into the soul, which lives for a very, very long time. It is like a vibration that goes out, endlessly, and such vibrations are either stimulated or reduced in power during human life. So every time the person responds to a positive or a good impulse, it is creating a better psyche or soul; in other words, it is creating good karma. Every time the soul refuses to respond thus, that good urge within the soul is losing ground, and the impulse for evil grows stronger. As the soul falters, it is like descending a mountainside, which it will have to climb again. The soul may attain a considerable height in its spiritual ascent and then, through lack of grip on the good, or failing to respond to some opportunity perhaps for service or kindness, it slips back a long way. We do not want to disturb you by giving these truths, but it is right that we should impart the knowledge that we have obtained.

In reincarnation, there are two things worthy of notice. One is that conditions of a former life are repeated again and yet again, and are also reversed. They are repeated and they are reversed. Once again we say, beloved brethren, that it is not only through the intellect that you can comprehend cosmic truth, but also by an inner awareness of vibrations built into the soul.

In this lies the secret of memory of past lives. Some people argue against the truth of reincarnation because they cannot remember their own past incarnations, and for this reason they say there can be no such thing as reincarnation. As we have pointed out, with each incarnation the soul has a fresh brain and the memory of its past does not lie in this brain, but in vibrations of the soul accumulated over many, many lives. Impulses and your reactions to conditions all create these vibrations within your soul. Memory of the past rests with the soul's ability to pick up these vibrations. When the soul becomes aware, the past begins to open up, because he or she can then feel certain soul-desires urging him or her to certain courses of action. The soul now begins to realize the reason behind these desires and those urges.

In meditation, remember, you must turn from the outer world, the world of action, to the inner world. In such periods of quiet, you gain growing understanding of why you have feelings telling you that you have perhaps been a soldier, a king or queen, a minister or priest or nun, a sailor, or a teacher in some past life. Moreover, you will find these urges actually working themselves out in your present incarnation. Therefore it is likely that the particular path that the soul follows—career, profession, or work—will bear some relation to a past incarnation.

As we have said, this tendency to repetition can be traced with each succeeding reincarnation. There will also be a tendency to reverse the action, which means that when a man or woman has lived in a fashion which may have caused pain and suffering to others, in a subsequent incarnation any suffering which has been inflicted will be reversed, so that precisely the same kind of suffering will return to him or her.

You may ask, is it possible for a soul to retrogress in any one incarnation? We would ask you this in turn. If one misses something beautiful on one's road, one often retraces many steps to find it. Would you call that retrogression?

It is utterly impossible for any one soul to judge another. To judge is self-condemnation. A soul may decide to enter the body of a drunkard in order to gain experience and discipline. You say, 'Oh, I would not choose that for myself!'. No, not while you are in this physical life, certainly. But who knows, when you can see from the higher worlds, you may decide to take a certain path because from that experience you will gain greater understanding of other souls. In the higher consciousness the soul is able to see perfectly clearly the lessons learnt or opportunities neglected.

The spirit is there from the birth, but the soul is in darkness until it responds to the stimulus of the spirit, until it becomes quickened by and aware of the spirit. The soul is the clothing of the spirit, and has a certain stimulus placed within it. This stimulus will enable it so to respond to what is called creative good that it will rise and be quickened by and unite with the spirit. There are many, many souls living in darkness at the present time. The Elder Brethren are trying by their love and help to awaken those 'dead' souls and bring them to life. The work of all the Great Ones, of the ages, is to help humankind to awaken from the sleep of death to the eternal life.

A question often arises about the 'disquieted spheres' —the lower astral plane. The natural process is for souls in the disquieted spheres sooner or later to rise from the suffering of those spheres, casting off the sheaths of denser matter, and so pass upward. There are cases when these souls cling so to the earth vibration that they do reincarnate quickly—but it is only just delaying the process of growth and evolution.

Many of you have said that reincarnation is so satisfying because it levels all people. You learn through reincarnation that all are brethren of the spirit, that she who was a queen yesterday (or in some previous life) may be a beggar today. He who was materially poor yesterday may be rich today. It teaches the true values of life as opposed to the false values of the world. It gives repeated opportunity to the soul for happiness, enjoyment, learning and all those things dear to the human heart. It reveals to you a God of love and justice.

Unless you study and strive and in the end fully comprehend the law of reincarnation, you cannot understand the purpose of life or cosmic truth, because without it there is no continuity of thought. The process of thought comes to a dead end. One short life with little or nothing accomplished seems hardly worth the while. When the soul is able to see its long, long journey, the ever-growing love and unification with the true companions of its spirit, life becomes beautiful. Any sorrow that visits the soul does not remain when the vision clears. That sorrow is a passing thing. The soul moves forward on its journey to greater and greater and more glorious experience. It is able then to understand happiness. It is able to feel the love of God. It is filled with hope because it knows that what has been withheld for a wise purpose in this incarnation will not be withheld for all time. The gifts of love are God's gifts to the soul.

# Chapter Five

## *The Seven Rays and Qualities of Consciousness*

THINK OF the first Great Cause, which perhaps it is easiest for you to conceive as the blazing, eternal spiritual Sun. Conceive within this Sun the triangle (symbolizing the trinity of many religions). These are the three who have always been since the beginning; who are concerned purely with the solar system and the evolution of the earth planet, and who are best understood as the three aspects, wisdom, love and power. These are the three from whom all life comes. From this trinity of wisdom, love and power comes also the angelic line of service, concerned with life in form throughout every kingdom.

Think again of the great cause, the Sun. See, now, from the Sun, the seven rays, the seven colours of the spectrum; the seven notes of music—for each note of music represents a colour and a cosmic ray—see the rays from the Sun, or this 'first principle', permeating all life and the whole universe. Each ray is connected with the Sun and all the angels of the rays work in the souls of people for the evolution, the growth and the gradual perfecting of the individual.

There are seven rays, and seven great beings, referred to in the Bible as 'the seven angels round the throne', who are called the Elohim, or the seven silent watchers at the head of their own particular ray. These rays are used to stimulate or assist humanity in its upward climb back to the central Sun, to the centre of life.*

Each of the Seven Rays upon which a soul progresses represents a planetary influence. You should think of the soul as the Sun, influenced by and influencing all the other planets in the solar system. This same interplanetary influence is in operation upon the human soul and through the many, many incarnations of its journey it is received again and yet again in different lives. This again is helping the Sun within the soul to open into greater brilliance and beauty. Throughout this planetary system we find the law of brotherhood, and even what appears to be conflict is resolving into harmony and perfection within the soul which it is assisting to grow. We often say that the divine plan is just, perfect and true. We say that all works together for good for those who love good or God. This is the law of the cosmos, even as gravity is a law of earth. All moves forward and upward.

You may wonder if the soul remains true to the one ray and works out its whole life on that one ray? The soul has to gain experience on all the rays but it

*The opening paragraphs of this chapter may also be read in White Eagle's WALKING WITH THE ANGELS, where there is further teaching on the Seven Rays.

clings to the one particular ray with which it is most in harmony. But that does not exclude it from experience on the other rays. The soul works for a long time on the one ray, but not exclusively. The soul in the course of its incarnations will have other experiences to prepare it. Eventually, after it has absorbed knowledge through its experiences on the other rays, all will blend into the one. The soul will then choose its particular ray because that ray gives it happiness and joy. As you advance on the path and pass through various initiations, you will find that all rays blend into one, into the white light, because the seven rays are as the seven colours of the spectrum. As you get nearer to the pure white light, you will find for instance that the rays of science, of teaching, of healing, and of music are all blended into one, and that the master soul has knowledge of all the rays.

Do you remember also the story of how the rainbow shone in the sky after the deluge? Will you think of the Master as being like that perfect rainbow, with all his vibrations perfectly unified, all the colours blending, not overbalanced, not underbalanced, but exactly balanced and perfect. The rainbow is the clothing of the Master, and when all these colours are blended perfectly, the pure white light is the result. And again, we draw the symbol of the Sun, or the Christ Light, shining upon the soul of man, which is the water (we use that term symbolically) and causing the breaking up of the colours into the rainbow. Thus through the sunlight or Christ light shining through it are seen the beautiful colours of the soul, of the perfect man–woman.

In certain great people, a quality of consciousness shines through. The light of the Sun will use a channel with the particular harmonious quality of consciousness that it needs to bring through on to the physical plane a certain truth, or to express beauty. I will try to illustrate this. I have in mind a master of a certain ray, the ray of ceremonial; a master who is reputed to have incarnated as certain well-known characters in history. I would show you that it is the soul-quality, the ray, which has incarnated in a series of different characters. Therefore to say that one individual was first so and so and then so and so, and to link up all the incarnations back through time, is both true and untrue. The individual soul in this instance responds to certain cosmic rays and vibrations. It corresponds to them, and therefore the soul will take the name that set of vibrations once had during the former life.

If every soul comes to the earth under a directing influence and is influenced by the planets, why does there need to be a system whereby we inherit qualities and limitations from our parents? The quality or the ray which the individualized soul of the child desires to express and develop is there in the particular parents chosen; in the quality of the soul of the parents, in their physical make-up, and in the environment. So what appears to be heredity is actually the set of conditions made ready for the planting of that seed in the exact soil it needs.

## *What, then, is Personality?*

 It is your own idea that each quality, each sign must be worked through in a separate incarnation. We want you to get away from the idea of separation, and think more of interblending, interpenetration of all these soul qualities. So we would say that the different states of consciousness can be worked through in one incarnation—not separately, but all at once. If you are going to reach the heart of the truth of life you have to get a comprehensive view of the whole. When folk declare they are Mary, or Peter, they forget there may be many incarnate on the earth expressing the same soul-quality, having that particular quality strongly emphasized.

The outer representation of reincarnation is confusing to those who think along certain lines. For example, the idea may be conveyed to you by a spirit guide that you are some personality that has lived before, perhaps in the days of Christ, perhaps in Egypt, and so forth. You think of yourself as that personality. Perhaps you yourself incarnated at the time of Christ. If I tell you that your name was Mary, you must not jump to the conclusion that you were Mary the mother of Jesus! We mean that you were then in incarnation, that that was the period of your output into the world. When I speak of your 'quality' of soul, I am linking that quality with names that have been used to identify certain qualities in history. Immediately you cling to a personality, to a particular person, you lose the real meaning of what you are.

Or let us suppose someone was told that he had once been called Peter. The human mind insists on jumping to conclusions—the human mind works upon the thought and clothes it, and creates a personality around it. Peter ... yes.... Perhaps *the* Peter? Yes, perhaps. And yet not the Peter who denied the Master, though the qualities of that soul-consciousness of *the* Peter may actually manifest in the present incarnation of the one named Peter.

So you will see that the outer presentation of reincarnation is an illusion, and yet true. You will have to get to work and find out what we mean, beneath that statement! You must interpret the outer life as representing the inner or soul-qualities. In meditating upon reincarnation, you will discover that reincarnation as generally understood is far removed from the truth. Therefore, when a teacher says, 'reincarnation is true; and reincarnation is not true', you don't know quite where you are!

Reincarnation in essence, in the mystical and esoteric sense, is a mystical truth. Reincarnation as usually understood is an illusion. I will make another attempt to explain. You must depart from the idea of separateness. On the physical plane all is working for separation. The mind likes everything cut and dried, everything beautifully labelled; and so the mind likes to think that it was once Joan of Arc, or Mary, Queen of Scots, or some other great name. The mind desires to know who it was, to put itself in a little parcel and label it, and say with precision, 'That is what I was. Now isn't this definite and satisfactory?'. Or if perhaps the past life was that of a villain, the mind delights to think, 'I was a bad lot!'. It loves to look at its own picture.

The mind, we tell you, works for separateness. But remember this, the mind is doing its work when it guides humanity towards individualization. Individualization up to a point appears to be separation, isolation. The mind works for the separateness and the individualization of the soul, the ego. That is its rightful function. However, as a person evolves he or she attains a finer individualization. Recognizing its individuality, it desires identification or unification with the whole, and will thus lose that sense of separateness. It will not lose itself, but actually identify itself with the whole. So instead of being an individual, small, compact, isolated, the soul becomes the universal; not separate from the greatness of the Mind of God.

Let us consider the twelve who were the disciples of Jesus, each one representing a certain soul-quality. We find, along the path of reincarnation, a John and a James, a Simon and a Matthew—each possessing, each radiating, soul-qualities (rays, if you like) of the one Sun. Who then are you? Do you know? You are John Smith or Mary Brown, you answer, but what does your answer mean? What is within? Not solely are you John

Smith or Mary Brown, but a great soul-impulse, which is being individualized and grows into the fullness of a perfect God-life. Behind all this, there is something so grand and beautiful, that all the little pettinesses and smallnesses of personality fade into insignificance.

In each incarnation a man or woman indeed has a distinct personality; but behind each of the personalities it chooses there dwells the same soul, and the sum of the experiences gained in those incarnations will be the true individuality. The personalities, although they merge harmoniously into the one grand consciousness, are nonetheless drops in the ocean, drops however that can always be separated. There is no such thing as death. An impression made on the ether is there for all eternity, like a thumb-print made on warm wax. The personality of Mr Jones is there for all time, but Mr Jones may not still exist, he may have outgrown himself. Each personality merges into one individuality. Yet we want you to understand that the personality will always be there, because nothing can ever be lost.

## Male, Female and Child

꙰We do not know gender in the same way as you know it. The soul chooses to incarnate in the kind of body that will enable it to gain the particular experience it is seeking. A wide margin of choice is given. The soul has free will within the law of God. It usually reincarnates with companions of its former lives because it has to come into contact with those to whom it owes debts. Every debt that is contracted in physical life has some day to be paid.

At this very moment of time you in the physical body are contracting karmic debts—a thought that is well worth retaining. This will reveal the opportunity that lies immediately before you. You can so order your lives that you do not contract bad debts because, as surely as night follows day, every bad debt must be faced in the future. This sounds like a threat. We do not mean it in this way, but it is the law. The wise man will respect the law and obey it in full. Life offers (when you recognize it) a grand opportunity. It is unwise to bemoan your fate or the particular conditions in which you find yourself in this incarnation. Rejoice, because difficulties are opportunities—opportunities for the development of the light within, for the strengthening of the building which is your soul. A wise teacher has said, 'Accept, accept life as it is'. Be deeply thankful for all experience because it offers opportunities for service to others and to yourself.

Of course, in a physical body you become so accustomed to the sex of that body that you cannot imagine yourself in a body of the opposite sex. You may not like the idea. What an old-fashioned outlook! Male and female are absolutely equal. This is a very vital truth, which must be realized on your earth. Until it is realized, until it is recognized in all the expressions of life on earth, equilibrium will not be restored. How can you expect progress, spiritual or material, when your ship is not on an even keel? Absolute equality as God created them, male and female, perfectly balanced, is one of the fundamental laws of life: equilibrium, balance, equality.

Some ask whether it is possible for one spirit or soul to incarnate in more than one body at a time? Nothing is impossible; but such a thing is, to say the least, very unusual. You have of course the example of the dual soul. That is an instance where the same soul will incarnate in two different bodies. There are cases where two aspects of the same soul will reincarnate separately—just as twins are born; but even twins of the same mother are not necessarily twin souls. Nothing is impossible, but certain things are not general.

Another example is the child that is stillborn, or who dies as a baby. It is not only the soul whose life is so short that is gaining experience, but the parents as well. No-one can live unto himself or herself alone. There can be no splendid isolation. All life is a most wonderful interpenetration, one soul with another in all of life's experiences. In this instance, the parents too are gaining experience, and the soul which lives in the flesh for only a few days gains later much experience on the astral planes immediately surrounding the earth. Occasionally a child who passed away as a baby will quickly return to the same family—for no hard-and-fast rule, as we have said, governs the time between incarnations.

## *Marriages, Groups and Friends*

❧Marriages, true marriages, are made in heaven. Are there many such ideal marriages on earth? Yes, there are some, and it is a state to which all people will attain eventually. Yes, the power behind life is responsible for your destiny; so may we very simply beg you to blame no-one who appears to have made an unhappy marriage? Certain alliances are brought about as a result of karma. Two souls may have debts to pay each other. They meet on earth, are irresistibly attracted. Just why, they do not know; they must come together. Then, apparently, they are very unhappy afterwards. Nevertheless both have been drawn together by an irresistible law and both must work out that condition before they can make spiritual progress. People do not have much choice in marriage. It is the power behind them which draws two people together—they do not choose, they cannot help themselves. It has to be.

You may incarnate at one time in a male body and at another in a female body. You may go on to ask whether it is then possible for two souls of the same physical sex to be affinities. We would answer like this. One aspect is the will; the other aspect of the complete ego is wisdom. Either may incarnate in either sex, if they have to gain certain experience, or for specified work requiring either a male or a female body. Always get behind the purely physical, outside covering, to the spirit. There you find the true individual.

Two people may be drawn together because they have a certain work to do; they may not necessarily be full spiritual affinities, but affinities insofar as they are harmoniously adjusted one to the other. Their joint work will help the race. The power behind humanity is always considering the whole human evolution, not merely individuals. We have all to learn that we are part of something else, not self-sufficient, and here marriage is a great teacher, because on this physical plane men and women learn through the marriage relationship the surrender of self—or should do. It does not matter what your partner does; it is your attitude to your partner that matters vastly to you. When the children of earth recognize this necessity for the sacrifice of self, and that there is no greater teacher than marriage, then they will indeed grow towards the divine love, the growth of which is the whole purpose of their creation.

We personally have seen a vision of life on the planet Venus where there is absolute expression of Divine Love and Divine Marriage, which has to be earned, which has to be attained through aspiration and work and service. When you are able to function on the true spiritual plane of your being, then you will realize what a state of darkness the earth is in, and how difficult it is for anyone who is enfolded and boxed in this earth condition to comprehend the glories of higher worlds.

You may ask whether, if we reincarnate in the same families, that means we continue to have the same parents, the same children? This is not exactly the case, but you are all drawn together in the same family. You are sometimes brother and sister, husband and wife, or father and son, and so on. According to the karma you have made you will find love and happiness or enmity and discord; this discord has to be moulded into love. Do not expect to get instant results when trying to give love. We know how difficult it is. Nevertheless love is the great unifier. Your work in this incarnation is to create love in your heart and a sense of sympathy and kindness even to those with whom you find relationships difficult.

An incarnating ego may be born into a family where a tendency to a certain physical affliction or disease exists, because that soul has certain work to accomplish, certain opportunities to be presented to it. That soul may or may not, according to its strength, take on that disease. That is a subtle point, because the soul need not succumb, but can so strengthen itself that it does not take that particular way of learning its lesson. We would not accept as a foregone conclusion what heredity seems to pass on, because every soul has within it the power to determine to a degree its method of working out its karma. A child may solve its sum in more ways than one, which is where free will comes in.

With regard to the group affinity, groups are drawn

together and work under the direction of the Lords of Karma. It is karma that decided the grouping of souls, and in reincarnation you will be born into a family or a group according to the karma you have earned in the past. And this applies also to one's friends. Every life is most accurately and perfectly planned according to the vibrations the soul has built into itself in the past. There is the most perfect organisation. Although there are millions and millions of souls at present incarnate, with every one of these children there is the perfect working out of the divine plan and pattern.

# Chapter Six

## *Responsibility for Each Other*

MANY SOULS are grieved at the thought that they might have to leave their loved ones. Many of you on earth are grieved at the thought of loved ones on the other side going forward without you. You think perhaps when you come to the spirit world you will find your friends already reincarnated? Well, it does not happen like that. You all move forward in groups. You move up the evolutionary path together in groups and in families.

In the ancient days, many drawn to the White Eagle Lodge were formerly together in the temple of the white light in Atlantis, where the worship of the great sun Ra was the religion of people and of the temples. Later you reincarnated in Egypt many times, because in those days Egypt was the great centre of light and learning after Atlantis was destroyed owing to the inequality of the white and black forces.* Those good brethren who were left knew that destruction was coming, so took the light and established it in the

*In MEMORIES OF REINCARNATION (formerly THE ILLUMINED ONES) a book which forms a useful companion to this one, Grace Cooke presents her own memories of times in ancient Egypt and the Andes. See above, p. viii.

ancient land of Khem, which is now called Egypt. That teaching of the brethren who settled in Egypt is to be found in your Bible, but all in allegory. Until you have the key you will not recognize or understand it in your Bible. But there it is. The teaching of Atlantis thus became that of the Egyptians; and many of the group at another time became Israelites. Do you see how the experience of the group unfolds?

Let us tell you of another way in which the group experience is repeated. The name 'Israelites' is another name for brethren of the sun, brethren of the light. From the Israelites, the Messiah is said to have been born. But, my brethren, all is a restatement of the ancient wisdom, the ancient Sun-worship, because the Messiah was the same Son of God whom we in the days of Atlantis worshipped, and did so again when he was known as Osiris. Today you call him Christ, but it was to that race—those people whom you call the Israelites—that the Sun was reborn for the western world; shall we say for a world which had become heathen, having lost the sacred word, lost the sacred mystery of life?

That you work in reincarnating groups is part of the divine plan. Do not reject the truth or wisdom of reincarnation because you are fearful of being separated from those you love, for in love there is no separation. You cannot be separated from any soul that is part of your soul, cannot be separated from those companions who move along the path of evolution with you—for you are as necessary to them as they to you. You reincarnate in families; you are drawn together either by the ties of darkness or light, either by what you call hatred or love. The whole purpose of spiritual evolution is for love to reign supreme and for all negative vibrations to be absorbed eventually into the positive good—which is all love, all wisdom, all power.

The more this subject is studied and understood, the surer becomes the conviction that the only way, the key to all action on earth, is love. It is kindness, gentleness. We know how right it seems to be to inflict punishment on the guilty, but the punishment is not to the flesh. The real punishment, or shall we say the lesson, is to the soul. That will come to the soul in course of time by the cosmic law, the law of God. Therefore the way of life is to be restrained, to be kind, and to have faith in the love and justice of God. *I will repay, saith the Lord.* The law of God is absolutely just, and when a person seems to suffer from injustice this is due to something that soul has once inflicted. It is only its own action coming back upon itself.

None of us can get away from divine law. In a sense this brings up another important and, we fear, controversial, point. We can only give you spiritual law and spiritual law is absolute justice. In this connection we must consider capital punishment. From the aspect of the spirit world, we know that it is not for humankind to take the life of the guilty party. Capital punishment must and will be abolished as people learn the wisdom of spiritual law. If a person violently takes the life of another, in course of time it will rebound upon him or her again. We say that capital punishment will not be a deterrent. What will stop the committing of these crimes is the increasing response of the soul to the light of God.

It is a very grave thought that all of us—we ourselves, and you who are in incarnation alike—are all responsible, to a degree, for all humanity. This is because our response to the good is going to help others to respond to good. Our lack of positive response—our laziness and our apathy towards spiritual things—has let the world down. The Master said, *I, if I be lifted up from the earth, will draw all men unto me.* This means that every individual is responsible to some degree for the suffering, darkness and crime in the world. You may not like this statement, but it is true.

*Ye cannot serve God and mammon*: another statement of the Master. It is so, so true. That is what we are endeavouring to impart. Once the soul in incarnation has seen the true way, that soul has a grave responsibility towards the rest of humankind. We cannot speak too earnestly on this subject. We do not preach to you. We are only speaking of those things which we have seen, which we have proven to ourselves; and the radiation of the light in your own lives, along with the establishment of centres of light, is of the gravest importance to the rest of humankind. It is the foremost work in the world at the present time. You and we carry a grave responsibility. What a privilege, what an opportunity have we earned, so to work for the light that all people may be illumined by the truth of the simple spiritual revelations of the Christ!

Someone once asked whether it was possible that we are sent into incarnation to affect the part of the world in which we dwell? The answer is *always*: that is the law. You cannot give without receiving. You are placed just where you are to give nourishment to the earth or physical plane of life, as well as to receive life from it.

There are many souls, particularly at the present time, who descend purely to help their younger brethren. For example, Jesus of Nazareth had incarnated before he became Jesus. Jesus of Nazareth was known in other forms. But do not confuse the Master with the Light or the illumination of the Son. The illumination shone in some degree through others, but please consider the idea of Jesus of Nazareth as an apex of the human incarnation. Therefore the illumination of the Christ manifested through his vehicle as never before on this earth plane.

We were once asked whether life might be likened to a sea or ocean that seems eternal, and human beings to waves, or to the tides that ebb and flow but are always part of the ocean? Those are very good similes. Life is always there, but it does not always manifest in the same conditions or through the same form of matter. You only know physical matter but there are other forms of life and other planets. *Life always is.* When you are on the crest of the wave you cannot see what is in the trough. That is true in human experience, but we are also thinking in terms of progress. We are thinking that life goes on and on up the spiral. It is impossible for the finite mind to conceive life in all its fullness; impossible to conceive infinity or eternity. Do not think in terms of life and death, because there is no death. Do not think that because a door closes another does not open. You pass from one condition of life to another. In your material problems never be anxious. Oh, how many times are we to tell you that! When one door closes another instantly opens. The trouble is that you like to have too many doors. You are not patient. You have to learn confidence in the eternal love and precision of the light. When a condition finishes never try to hold on to it. Always move forward.

## Reincarnation and Karma

❧It is a psychic law that at all times you and all humankind are making impressions on the Akasha, or the higher ether. We who are disembodied are able to find you by your record! Now, don't let this frighten you, rather be thankful that you are dear and very near to spiritual guides and angelic guardians.

'You require to learn certain lessons, my brother or my sister', the voice says. 'This life will bring you into contact with this or that soul, with whom you have contracted a karmic debt.' There are alternative paths shown also. The soul can choose which path it takes. There are many, many opportunities that the soul has of working out its salvation. You find it difficult to believe that your troubles, as you call them, are of your own making? Then your nose is too close to the picture. Nevertheless the pattern of the life is one you have made for yourself, by your past actions and because of your spiritual aspiration. So you get two pulls—that of your past karma (which is what one might call the negative) and also of your spiritual aspiration, that pull of your soul to God. But over all these conditions, love is the ruler.

You may ask if it is possible to shorten one's karma by doing one's best in whatever circumstances one is placed. We would answer, assuredly—this is part of the divine secret which the soul learns. Do your best. Be tranquil and calm. 'To thine own self be true', as your poet says. That is the answer. Be true to that inner light.

We would also say this. Accept the circumstances of your life, knowing that they are placed there by a God of wisdom and love. Even if the circumstances are difficult and painful, meet them calmly. Do your best. Then you will, as you call it, shorten your karma. You will not be creating fresh karma and you will be paying off karmic debts of the past. You move forward to a state of liberation from all karma, when the need for rebirth is removed. The soul progresses into more glorious states of life when it has passed through conditions in this world and has attained a degree of mastership over matter. That is the purpose of mastership—becoming master of all emotions and mental limitations and so forth. When the soul has attained complete mastery, it passes onwards, upwards into more glorious states of existence. Until it has learned mastership it can neither comprehend nor see, and nor can it enter into those higher states of being. Before you all is the path of attainment. It will lead you to happiness and beauty such as you have never glimpsed.

A further question occurs as to whether it is possible to work out karma in the one life or whether you must wait until another incarnation? Again, we would say that most certainly, you can work out karma in the one life. Karma often comes back very quickly. For instance, if you neglect your duty to the laws of health, you suffer. Your karma will overtake you. It is not necessary for karma made in this life to be carried forward into a next life. The bigger the deed, the wider is the circle that is affected.

You may have heard it said that many now living will not have to reincarnate. You may wonder at this, since it is a common belief that all karma had to be worked off before a soul is freed from rebirth. However, at the present time there is a speeding-up of evolution, and there will be many who will be given other duties—I will put it in that way. It does not mean that you will leave some debts unpaid. Rather you will have other ways of paying, still in connection with earth humanity.

There are those of you, also, who may have been puzzled by the fact that some eastern religions teach the eradication of desire of any kind, or the attainment of desirelessness so that the soul can reach *nirvana*. Because it has freed itself from desire (so the teaching goes) it makes no more karma, and it thereby escapes the ceaseless round of birth and death or reincarnation.

This may suit some people, but others would perhaps wish to come back, to help or to serve. We would say in answer that in different religions you get a different presentation of truth, the one that is the particular kind of teaching acceptable by humankind at that particular age. Perhaps nowadays you see a truth given in some previous age from a higher aspect. You comprehend a little better, then, the meaning of that past religion. Truth is like a jewel with many facets. There are many paths to God. Someday when all the varying religionists arrive at their goal, they will be amazed to find all their friends there also. The main lesson is to live and let live. Do not interfere with other people for they have their particular path to God. Say, 'God bless you. My love is with you as you journey'. The sage will never try to force anyone against their will. The sage just smiles and keeps very still. Having seen truth, the sage sees that his brother, or her sister, will also find truth—some day.

Finally, supposing one soul does another a great

wrong, and the wronged soul has sufficient knowledge, love and understanding completely to forgive? With the wronged one bearing no resentment and loving that soul, does that finish off the karma? We will answer that question by drawing your attention to the great wrong that Judas apparently did when he betrayed his Master and for an unworthy reward. He sold his Master. But Jesus forgave Judas. He drew the karma away from a lesser soul. We mean by this that Judas had to go through that particular experience of betraying his Master—in other words it was his karma. A lesser soul than Jesus would have retaliated in a later life, but because Jesus drew Judas's karma upon himself Judas was forgiven, because Jesus was what he was.

We have gone a long way round to give you a simple answer, but we wanted to make it clear. Jesus forgave Judas his karma. He helped that soul forward by his forgiveness, but when Judas came to his senses he still suffered and he learned through suffering. No other soul was involved, so when a soul can pay back a debt with love, that soul is not only helping the person who wronged him or her but many others also, because he or she is breaking a whole train of karma involving many, many other souls.*

So it is a very great act for any human being to be able to forgive his or her enemies. Jesus said, *Love your enemies.* This is the reason why you should: it is not only

*For a fuller treatment of the story of Judas, see chapter 13 of White Eagle's book THE LIVING WORD OF ST JOHN.

that you thus help one particular soul, but also that one act of love and forgiveness cuts short the resulting karma which would involve many others. It is like handing somebody a receipted bill. It means there is nothing to bind you but love if you meet in the next life—not necessarily a strong link, but one of gentle brotherhood and beauty. Forgiveness is the greatest thing in the whole world. Jesus taught it again and again and again. *Pray for them that despitefully use you. Love your enemies.* Forgive those who hate you, who have hurt you. That is what it all means. Forgive … forgive. Just let everything fall away. And do not retain any sneaking feeling of goodness or piousness, as the Pharisees did!

We do not criticise any soul. All of you have your own particular work to do. You are in the very place to which you have been led by your guide or by cosmic law. Sometimes that is a strange place, and though you have responsibility for your actions, there still may be times when you do not understand what has urged you to act. If only you would always remember this, that even if your actions seem to you in retrospect not to have been right, there was a power guiding you. You do what the law bids you to do because you are so associated with that law. You are part of cosmic law, and therefore you by your very life are fulfilling God's law. But remember, whatever you are called upon to experience, to be humble and thankful. Accept, accept, accept all that has to be, knowing that it is the outworking of the law, the law of cause and effect.

Every one of you has to undergo a crucifixion, such as Jesus suffered, in your own inner self. You have to learn by self-discipline and by the discipline placed before you by the Laws of Karma and Reincarnation. In each successive life, you move a little way forward. You may not appear to do so, but appearances are very deceptive. All the while there is this continual, slow, progressive turning of the wheel, this coming into a physical body to accept karmic lessons, this outgoing from the physical body to a place of refreshment. We emphasize this: *to a place of refreshment.*

When you can recognize this grand truth of life, you will understand the reason for each experience, and not shrink from any one of them. You will look at each and say, 'Now what have I got to learn from this? I must have neglected something in the class below, so I have got to go through this again and learn the lesson which I missed'. For life is a great geometrical problem, set by the Grand Geometrician, and you will find that every tiny episode and experience fits into place. Nothing happens by chance or mischance. Everything is working out according to the divine plan.

Your freewill choice lies not in your lower mind, but in the directing power and the inward light of yourself. You may react to certain experiences, absorbing the good, or you may just be lazy—like a naughty child at school who won't do the lesson, so gets a black mark. If you shirk, the same old lesson will come up again and again and again until at last it is learnt.

You will recognize the truth of this, because if you carefully scrutinize your own life, you will see that every experience that comes to you tends to teach one and the same lesson. Lessons have to be mastered, you have to be perfected, and the purpose of incarnation is that the individual soul may be perfected. You are made perfect through physical experience.

Can a man or woman gain experience in the spheres after death? To some extent, on the astral plane, yes; but not entirely. The mortal body is the way you yourself have chosen. You must learn your lesson through your mortal, fleshly body. When you rise above the limitations of the flesh, you will no longer need this fleshly body, and you will then pass on to other realms of life, to other planets, where there are forms of life not yet understood.

Oh, a grand panorama of life awaits you, when you recognize the true purpose of life! When you recognize that incarnation is to teach you to become a master of the flesh; a master of the astral, a master of the mental plane! Then, at last, there will come freedom from rebirth.

## Past Lives and Healing

&rarr;All disease commences in the soul, in the etheric body; and the soul body, or the seed of the soul body, is carried from one incarnation to another. You make a fresh start, with a clean slate, in each incarnation, but unless you have caught the vision and are obeying the law of God in the way you live, the way you think, and the way you act, you are creating fresh karma every day. The karma sometimes is shown to you very quickly, but on other occasions it just rests within your soul. Your soul, when it leaves your physical body and passes on into higher spheres, carries on the impression of the karma that you have made in your life, and all the karma is gathered up into a permanent seed-atom.

Now that seed-atom is the part that comes back in every incarnation, and you have to contend with that basic karmic condition. Remember that that karmic condition can be transmuted or cleared by your life in the present, by your attunement to the God-life. It is as simple as this: by your love, the love you can engender in your innermost being every day of your life, your karma can be transmuted. The more you can increase your love for all creation, the more you can attune yourself to the light of Christ, the more you are transmuting your karma.

Many ancient races recognized the subconscious mind as the seat of many diseases. The so-called witch doctor, who had special knowledge, would get to work on the subconscious of the patient and would bring out and release all kinds of inhibitions. Not all, however: certain things could not be accounted for. Our modern psychologists find themselves helpless on occasion, too; although even then, they may try to build up some sort of explanation. If psychologists could only understand the laws of karma and reincarnation, they would see that these conditions may be due to memories in the physical body shared by the whole race, and they may also be auric memories: that is, ones held in the aura of the patient.

For instance, a person may, long ages past, have created certain karma through wrong deeds, ill thoughts, maybe through lust for power. Perhaps certain so-called black forces are attached to him or her because he or she has used them in the past, unknowingly. This person will have attracted to him or herself elementals—which, strange as it may seem, have a very long life. These past conditions, what we will call 'pre-conscious' states, return to the soul when it reincarnates. The evils attracted to and stored up in the aura, the evils created by the individual in the past, return in subsequent incarnations; and then they have to be faced, they must be expiated.

We are told that after being accused of healing on the Sabbath, Jesus later met in the temple the man he had healed at the pool of Bethesda—and our interpretation is that Jesus raised his vibrations, and that he met the man made whole in some temple on the inner planes. Have you yourselves not, during meditation, entered such a temple: your temple on the inner planes? Even thus, Jesus met the soul of the man he had healed, and spoke with him, just as he may speak with you on the inner planes. *Sin no more*, said Jesus, *lest a worse thing come unto thee.* Note how Jesus, by this act, was affecting the karma of those whom he healed. Right up to the moment of the crucifixion, he performed miracles, acted with a supreme compassion and love, drawing to himself the karma of those he saved. In this case, the patient was indebted to Jesus for his healing; therefore karma was created. But Jesus would not exact payment. Most people exact payment to the very last ounce.

So, if you can give back love, you will expiate your karma. Jesus thus affected the karma of many while on his mission. He has been affecting the karma of the world ever since. The karma of the world is being gradually changed through love of Christ; this is the transmutation of karma through love.

Do you not see that when Jesus performed a miracle and healed a physical body, such a cure was only for a brief time, and not for eternity—only for the span of the earth life—if the soul of that person failed to respond further? Unless the soul responded in fullness to the divine love, it could not escape the judgment of reincarnation—for the reincarnating soul confronts its judgment in life after life in the karma allotted to it. When there is no more reincarnation, then a soul has met its judgment in the divine love that arises and glorifies it.

# PART II

# LIVING ONE
# LIFE AMONG MANY

# Chapter Seven

## *Healing Guidance*

A SPIRITUAL healer who is attuned to God is able to bring to the patient the stimulus of the love ray, the power of love. Healing is really by love. When we say love, we mean dynamic love—the Will of the Father being expressed through the Son, through the healer. *The Father that dwelleth in me, he doeth the works.*

   In the past, the healer would call upon the subconscious or the psyche of the patient, call to it and talk to it. That is what psychological healing is doing today. But also, just as you can talk to the subconscious, you can also call to the Christ within to quicken, to raise the patient from the dead. But of course this can only be done by one who has reached a stage on the path where he or she is qualified to do so. You may like to think of the body as composed of so many atoms or cells, and that in each cell is a spark of God that can be called upon to perfect the body.

   True love is the key, the secret. All wise men and women, all the saints, know this. You will find throughout the ages that the key lies in the heart. The key is simple love, true love: but not an emotional gushing forth! That is not love; love is the will of the Father–

Mother. Love is *doing* the will of the Mother–Father which sent you: that is the key.

There is such a thing as spiritual guidance, not only through the innermost being, not only through the inner light, but guidance by guides, wise friends, or guardian angels in the beyond. The spirit guide helps because the guide has a clearer vision than either the healer or the patient; the guide can inspire and tell the healer what method a particular patient requires. The guide can help the healer by directing the hands, by directing the rays, and also by talking to the subconscious of the patient. Yes, the guide does a lot of work in healing, in collaboration with the healer and the patient!

Many are responding unconsciously to such guidance. The time will come when all of you will respond to your guardian angel. By then, humans and angels will walk side by side on earth. *Ask, and it shall be given you*—ask for guidance, particularly as you fall asleep at night, and be on the alert for impressions in the early morning. Answers will be dropped into your minds. You will be amazed at the true guidance and help forthcoming. In time, your guide will become known to you as a very much loved companion. Every one has a guide, but not every one has open eyes, nor open ears.

Many of you are very puzzled and ask, 'Who are my guides?'. 'Why is it that sometimes a guide is described as an American Indian, sometimes as an Egyptian, sometimes as Chinese; sometimes, perhaps, as a Greek?' So you say, 'Well, I seem to have a great number of guides!'. Has it occurred to you that your guide may be expressing him- or herself according to the vibration of the moment? The guide may choose to be clothed in a Chinese astral form, or as an ancient Egyptian, and so forth. We suggest that in the temple of every soul there lie many cloaks or dresses.

Remember that the divine spirit, or the light, as it comes down from those celestial spheres (or shall we say, as the light comes from within to express itself on the outer planes?) may select any one of the astral dresses. It comes forth as an expression of the spirit, and in order to contact the earthly vibrations at all, it must clothe itself with a selected body, which is reassembled and used by the spirit for its work on or near the physical or astral planes of life.

## *Right Thought, Right Action, Right Living*

❧Three points we now have in mind. The first is right thought; the second is right action; and the third is right living. The last two rest upon the foundation of the first point, right thought. The power of thought, the extent of the influence of right thought, is beyond human comprehension. Of course, right thought is always based upon God; it is God-thought, good-thought. You have heard the saying that thoughts are things. What you think today, you become tomorrow.

You thus daily create or re-create your body, your life, your soul, and build your spiritual achievement, through right thought. Many people will not accept this and make no effort to discipline their thought, for it requires self-discipline. When we say this, many questions will come crowding into your mind, particularly into the lower mind, tending to deny the truth of our statement. But remember the importance of a steady 'keeping on keeping on'. It is the one who sees his or her goal and works towards it that attains both perfection and happiness.

While good thought is our ideal, it can only be put into practice according to your state of development, according to the laws that govern your life. We must recognize and submit in humility to the cosmic laws of reincarnation and of karma (or cause and effect).

It is not easy for the average person to recognize profound and fundamental truth, particularly when he or she is functioning through the limitation of the earthly mind. A person must probe deeper than the ordinary mind in order to glimpse the justice as well as the love demonstrated in the law of reincarnation. Through reincarnation, you have the opportunity of fulfilling the law of cause and effect, although you do not necessarily have to reincarnate. We mean by this that you do not necessarily work out your karma in your next life or in your several future lives. You may be working out your karma of yesterday today. You may have sown the seeds of your present state of ill-health, or of your unhappiness and maybe disturbed and unruly emotions in this present life, several years ago. Now you are reaping what you have previously sown. You must not blame God for these things. You must look within; examine yourself humbly and honestly and admit mistakes when you see them. If you cannot recognize your own weaknesses, pray that you may soon be shown them.

We do not say anything in harshness. We come back in order to help you, not to judge you, nor to condemn anyone. We come with love, to offer you wisdom gained by experience.

Now the first commandment is: *Thou shalt love the Lord thy God with all thy heart, and with all thy soul, and with all thy mind.* You shall love good and you shall be one-pointed in your love for God. This brings us back again to our first point, God-thought. Your life should be lived in God-thought, with the thought of good, looking for good, believing in good, trusting in good, constantly holding good thought about life generally, and about your neighbour. You must live always seeing the better, the good side, never the negative. You will be surprised at what will result. When you feel little aches and pains, instead of encouraging and nurturing them, put in their place a perfect thought, a God-thought. We know that this is a gospel of perfection, but we also know that until you put this into daily practice, you will continue in muddle and confusion.

We are giving you principles. The first is: always

think well, always think good, eschew evil and all negative things. Seek only for God, for good in your thoughts.

Now for the next point: put right thought first. Control thought, thinking what you will to think, not letting thought run riot. Control it, train it, direct thought by power of the spirit, the holiness which is deep within your soul. When the thoughts are controlled and directed rightly towards God, there must come a natural prompting towards right action. If the thought be right, the act must be right. Right action is God action.

## *By what Principles shall we Live?*

☙If you study the lives of the saints and mystics, even in so-called modern times—let us say within the last six thousand years or so—you will find that all these people lived simply, were very careful about what they ate and what they did. They lived in extreme simplicity. They ate the fruits of the earth. The true Illumined Ones did not eat meat.

Now questions have been put to us, such as, 'White Eagle, we wish you would give us a lead as to whether we should all become vegetarians. We wish you would tell us what we should think about capital punishment, what we should think or do about surgical operations, and what is our right attitude towards war?'

Although you put them to us, many such questions

come pressing in upon anyone who walks the spiritual path. Your Bible says, *Thou shalt not kill.* The words mean exactly what they say! You cannot juggle about with such words; they are quite plain. The great Lord Buddha also taught his disciples never to take life, to regard life as sacred and holy. God alone gives life. Have you any right to take the life of another, ever? We leave it to you to answer your own question.

We know that your Bible also says, *An eye for an eye and a tooth for a tooth* and so on; does this mean a life for a life? We think you will find that such sayings mainly refer to the law of karma, which works out exactly, but you yourself set the law in action. You should regard life as God-given and holy and should not take the life of any creature. However, we must still recognize that humankind has descended from a high estate, come down through the planes into matter for a purpose, so that people may learn to realize in matter the Source of their life, and develop the indwelling seed-atom of Christ until it grows into the full consciousness of the divine being.

Present-day humanity is imprisoned in earthliness, in materialism—we are going to say, in 'animalism'—and therefore cannot change instantly; but humankind can still have an ideal and can work towards it. Evolution is always a slow process, but when this inner light quickens, it works in the human conscience. The body will pull hard against the spirit, being of the dust of the earth and with animal instincts. Therefore it will argue with you and say to you, 'Oh, but I must eat animals. Indeed I must! I shall not be healthy if I don't'—which is of course nonsense. Life is maintained by living on the fruits of the earth. It does not need the flesh of another creature. Then the old argument crops up: 'But if you eat a lettuce or if you eat only fruit, you are hurting something. This must be as bad as killing an animal'.

No! You can eat the fruits of the earth because they grow on the earth from its substance, from its dust in order to feed human life. Vegetation has not the same consciousness as is possessed by an animal. But apart from this, remember the blood that is shed when an animal is killed. If you were offered a cup of this blood you would probably be repulsed. No civilized person could drink its contents because they would be revolted. The very thought revolts you. We say that until humankind feel a like revulsion at the thought of eating the flesh of animals, they will continue to eat it. But the Illumined Ones would never do this, and humankind must inevitably reach the point where to eat the flesh of animals is impossible.

The next question is naturally, 'Is war permissible?'. We fear that our answer will not be very palatable. We know that the earthly mind puts forward many reasons why war should continue, but from the higher aspect of life, humankind should never participate in war. Think about something else: the idea of eating human flesh would be so abhorrent that you cannot bear the thought of it. Carry this thought to a logical conclusion, and you would know that one human should never slay another, even in self-defence. It is of no use to put problematical instances before us and ask, 'Well, if someone ran in and wanted to kill a person I love—should I not naturally stand up to them?'. These hypothetical cases prove nothing. You cannot judge a question like this from a hypothetical case because you do not know what you would do or how you would react in given circumstances. Better to abide by the plain law, *Thou shalt not kill.*

As we have often said before, so long as humankind lives by slaying and eating animals, so long shall humankind be slain by others and wars will continue. It is wrong to kill any form of animal life. Abolish wrong action. Right action is to revere life, to regard life as God's gift.

Now we feel other questions coming, such as, 'Are we permitted to kill a fly—or a mouse?'. You must really be sensible. The thing is, what you have to do, do quickly, and do painlessly, as Jesus said. We would go a little farther and say that when you are always putting right thought into operation there will be no pests. All these annoyances come because you yourself are annoying to each other. So, will you remember? Live rightly, think rightly, act rightly, and there will be no more killing of any kind. We would go so far as to say there will no longer be need for the surgeon's knife when humankind lives in accordance with divine law.

And the bloodstream, too—we are answering a question we hear on the ethers—the bloodstream is a holy thing, closely allied to the spirit, to the God within. 'Is blood transfusion permissible?', someone is asking. At the present time, a blood transfusion has long been the means of saving many lives. Nevertheless, from a spiritual or esoteric aspect, the mingling of the blood has certain occult risks. We would not go so far as to say, 'Refuse it', but it is one of those things that will be disposed of in time.

When there is right thought, right action, right living, all these crude methods will be unnecessary. Other forms of healing will develop, if healing is necessary—which we doubt, because when once humankind has attained to right thought, right action, right living, each can heal him or herself. We shall be able to recreate the temple of our bodies. This is what the masters have already done. They have demonstrated for you the result of right thought. They have lived harmoniously. Their needs have been supplied. Divine law feeds everyone. Did not Jesus refer to the lilies in the field? Did he not say that God is aware of the need of His–Her child? *The very hairs of your head are all numbered.*

If you are putting the Law of God into action in your life, you will be fulfilled. We do not tell you to sit down and say, 'Now, God, feed me, clothe me, house me; I am just going to enjoy myself'. If you have earned the right to do that, through a life of service, God will undoubtedly look kindly upon you. But no-one can live unto himself or herself. If you are not physically active, you can be spiritually active and continually send forth rays of life and light and goodwill which will bless and uplift all humankind.

As Christ said: *If I be lifted up, I will raise all men unto me.* No life is lived unto itself. A good life has an influence and effect upon many lives. One person living in total isolation can send a great light out to the world. Even today there are people who live the life of a saint: people who apparently do little but are a great influence for good. They pray; they heal; they uplift; they inspire; they create beauty, harmony, and surely such a creation is the work of God working through God's human child.

We hope these words will give some basis upon which you can think and reason, and on which to build. Yet we know that this is only touching the fringe of wisdom and knowledge.

# Chapter Eight

## *Overcoming Limitations and Finding Wings*

SOME OF YOU will know of a play called 'The Blue Bird'.* In it, the bird escaped from captivity, and the children who loved the bird passed through many adventures in their search for their blue bird. Eventually, it returned to them of its own free will. They prepared, unknowingly, for its return, and it returned.

In this play, one can trace the journey of the soul in search of God. The soul passes through adventures or initiations; it learns lessons from both suffering and happiness. In the play of the blue bird, we can read the deepest teachings on reincarnation—on life, death, and rebirth. We can realize the lesson it teaches: that simple truth of living in the place in which God has placed us, of loving and giving happiness to others.

The Ancient Wisdom frequently made use of birds as symbols to teach certain lessons to the aspirant, to the neophyte. Those familiar with the Ancient Wisdom, and with the teachings of Freemasonry, know that certain birds are to be found continually in the

*'The Blue Bird' is a play by the Belgian author, Maurice Maeterlinck (1862–1949), at one time very popular in esoteric circles in Britain.

mysteries; each bird representing a soul-quality or qualities which the neophyte is seeking. Birds in ancient days were considered to be messengers of the gods, and to simple-hearted folk a bird was thought a very wonderful creature, because it usually lived in the sacred forests and groves and flew from tree to tree singing melodious, joyous songs. These were interpreted by the people to be voices of the gods, speaking to the human soul.

Moreover, bird life was a source of great wonder because birds were free to fly; they possessed the secret of levitation. Birds had overcome the power of gravitation, which is a law of earth. Levitation is a law of the spirit.

May we explain that at a certain stage in his or her training the neophyte learns to use spiritual wings to move about the spirit worlds freely? This happens both when he or she quits the physical body after death, and also when the neophyte is being trained to vacate the physical body during his or her physical lifetime and to move about the spiritual worlds freely. The neophyte learns to overcome the illusory law of gravity. If people could comprehend the spiritual law of levitation, they could transport themselves from one side of the world to the other—a practice frequently accomplished by the masters. When the neophyte is being thus trained for flight on the astral plane, he or she has to learn to overcome fear of falling and learns to fly in spirit life, as do the birds. The neophyte was often taken to a great height, from which he or she had to descend. Everyone has to experience within themselves the overcoming of gravitation: to learn that in the astral or soul body one can move about anywhere with ease.

This will explain why the initiates or students of the spiritual mysteries regarded birds with adoration and respect. They were creatures drawn to the central life-force of the Father–Mother God, and as such were holy and had a message for humankind. Each bird in flight demonstrated to the neophyte the desired quality of spiritual attainment.

In the ancient mysteries, the neophyte was taught that he or she must die, must lose all that was of the lowest self; that the outworn life of materialism must go, must be completely erased. This did not mean that the physical body itself had necessarily to die, but that the lower particles of that physical body had to disintegrate before the new spiritual body could be formed. This may be one of the interpretations Jesus had in mind when he said, *Except a man be born again, he cannot see the kingdom of God.*

The phoenix is a mythical bird that clearly depicts this profound spiritual truth. The eagle has sometimes been confused with the phoenix, but we would suggest to you that the eagle and the phoenix share very similar symbolism. The eagle is generally regarded as the national symbol of America. Those composing the New Race are being drawn from various countries both in the East and the West. The central point will be in the new world in the West—America. The Atlantis that was is again to be reborn. The actual continent, will it rise again? Not exactly. We rather mean that the ancient power and wisdom of the Atlanteans will be again established on earth. Realize then the many, many years it takes to bring to birth this New Race, or this spirit of the reawakened human being.

There is an interesting story about the Great Seal of the United States of America. When that Great Seal was being planned, behind the statesmen were the Rosicrucian Brotherhood; that ancient Brotherhood which was in existence at the very beginning of life on earth. By no accident was the eagle chosen one of the symbols of the Great Seal. You see the meaning? The bird with wings—to enable it to overcome the law of gravity, materialism; a creature with wings—to soar into the heavens and to receive the guidance, even the command, of the Wise Ones who watch over humanity.

There is evidence to prove that a brother, one of the Sages, actually manifested in a physical body at the conference table at the time of the formation of the US constitution. So you will begin to glimpse the wondrous foresight of the Sage, and the length of preparation that ushers in a new spirit, a new age. For many centuries past brethren of the Ancient Wisdom made preparations in America for this wondrous coming.

Birds have a great significance. You can learn from listening to the birds, observing their plumage, their ways of life, their haunts, to translate their song into spiritual harmony and truth. We say, 'I am happy as a bird'. Can you imagine a birdless world? What makes a lonely place so beautiful to the traveller? No matter how anxious you are about earth conditions, if you can be carried away by their music, you know happiness, you know joy, and at the same time you know the emotion you call sorrow.

## *The Tree Cycle*

❧ The Master Jesus referred more than once to trees—and he cursed the barren fig tree, an action that has remained a puzzle to many Christians. He cursed the fig tree because it bore no fruit, and by so doing he showed to us that a person must bring forth the fruits of life, and that if he or she fails through sloth or ignorance to bring forth the fruits of life, this incarnation is nil, is wasted. Like a tree, the individual life must not be barren of good, nor wholly unproductive.

The trees have ever been recognized as symbols of the mysteries. The oak, by its strength and endurance, was known to some as the symbol of the great Father–Mother God; the ancient sages worshipped beneath its shelter. The pine tree, graceful and worshipping, has ever been symbolical of the Son of God.

The trees are symbolic of birth and death, and also of reincarnation. They manifest life at the right season, and shed their leaves at the waning of the sun. They also pass into abeyance and quietness, they withdraw before they once more put forth their energy to add fresh growth; they pass from rest to labour, and so to rest again—ever the rhythmic cycle of life. Sun-worship, to which this is linked, perhaps may have been crude in method, but remember that behind these ancient rites was a universal secret of life and creation. Is it not understandable then, that the man Jesus was hung upon a tree? The tree is a symbol of his passing; and a symbol too of the death of the man, the death of the human (the limited and physical) self, and the rebirth or resurrection of the spirit.

The mysteries gradually became withdrawn, and the spiritual life became buried deep within the earthly soul (even as the roots of the trees go deep for nourishment, energy and strength); and so the reminder the trees can offer has become forgotten. You may regard the rites and symbols of the ancient ones as crude, and even idolatrous, yet if you had understanding you would have reverence and respect.

# Chapter Nine

## *The Church, the Bible, Jesus and Reincarnation*

IF REINCARNATION is true, some will ask, why is it not made clearer in the teachings of the Christian church? Let us think for a few moments about the history of western Christianity. If we look back fifteen hundred years and more we find dissension amongst the Fathers of the church about its doctrine. At this point we would digress for a few moments to mention that a great deal of the early Christian teaching came from the ancient teaching of Sun-worship, and was drawn from the Ancient Wisdom and the mystery schools of Greece and Egypt, India and the Far East, and also from the western brotherhoods which have always existed in remote places. There is no new truth. Cosmic truth remains. It always has been: *as it was in the beginning, is now and ever shall be.* Cosmic truth from time to time is freshly revealed to men and women according to their state of receptivity, according to the state of the soul's growth and aptitude to receive it. So we find at the foundation of the Christian church the Ancient Wisdom.

Even right after the days of the master Jesus,

there was dissension about the actual presentation of these truths, a tendency to lose sight of the mystical teaching of Jesus and his disciples (especially St John). The Fathers of the early Christian church gave their interpretation, but then throughout history there has ever been a tendency to misinterpret or misunderstand the spirit of the teacher. *The letter killeth but the spirit giveth life.* This means that the word of mouth can be easily misunderstood, but the light of the heart never, because it is the truth. So we begin to see that it is the life of the person and not their words which gives the truth. Love and light that flows from the heart is true. As soon as organisation steps in and committees and councils and so forth take a hand, then the light of the spirit recedes and is lost in a sea of words and organisation.

So also the true teaching of reincarnation seems to have been lost to orthodoxy through people's desire to wield political and national power. By reason of this the sweet, simple and true teachings of the Cosmic Christ, as spoken by the master Jesus, were lost sight of. We do not say that it was not necessary. All we are endeavouring to do is to show how the pure light of the Cosmic Christ can be buried beneath the mists of earthly thought, intrigues and the desire for power and possession. Nevertheless, in your Christian Bible—for those of you who can read it by the light of your innermost spirit—the truth of eternal life and of reincarnation still remains.

Jesus, the master, made a clear reference to reincarnation when he said that John the Baptist was Elias (Elijah). There is a similarity between the history of Elijah and of John the Baptist. Remember what we said about the tendency for the reincarnating soul to repeat itself. Both characters spent their time between the desert and the king's palace. The first was fed in the desert by ravens; John the Baptist also wandered in the wilderness, and tried to feed men and women by giving them the word of God. In one incarnation, he was fed physically and in the next given spiritual food.

At the present moment we have in mind this soul through whom our messages are transmitted [Grace Cooke]. Once, in a past incarnation, this woman taught a small group of children. Shall we say that we were teaching, because even in those days there was collaboration between the one in spirit and the one on earth. Now we are again imparting knowledge. Again the repetition of a previous life.*

So also in the case of Elijah and John. Elijah, although he did not always respond to the impulse of divine love because he persecuted the priests of Baal, in his next incarnation as John suffered persecution in his turn from Herodias, and by the princess at whose request he was beheaded. This was the working out of his karma. The severity once inflicted in his incarnation as Elijah returned to his incarnation as John.

*The story is told in her book MEMORIES OF REINCARNATION. See Introduction, p. viii.

We will also illustrate what we mean by referring to the parables of Jesus, because, contrary to the belief of many people, the master Jesus taught reincarnation. One parable was about a man who was in debt to a just and good master who forgave him his debt. That same debtor, as a creditor to a far lesser degree, would not forgive those who owed him debts. Because he would not forgive his debtor's debts, that man was bound. So he had to return—to reincarnate, in other words. He was put into the prison of reincarnation, into physical life until he should learn forgiveness.

In the Lord's Prayer are these words: *Forgive us our trespasses as we forgive those who trespass against us.* This same law works out through life after life, through incarnation after incarnation, until the soul has learned the lesson of love, kindness and forgiveness. It does not make any difference what you believe. It is what you are in your actions towards other human beings, to animals, and to life itself, that matters.

Another parable tells us about the unjust steward who robbed his master, but to the benefit of other people. *The children of this world are in their generation wiser than the children of light.* That seems an extraordinary thing for the Master to have said. This parable tells us that the unjust steward, although dishonest enough to rob his master, at the same time showed kindness and generosity to others. Because of this, and in spite of his dishonesty to his master, he was nevertheless due to reap some reward in the next generation, or the next incarnation—for we interpret 'generation' to mean 'incarnation'.

This important parable teaches us that the things the world considers sinful, such as dishonesty and the sins of the flesh, are not so great in the eyes of God as the sins of unkindness and cruelty. There are people on your earth who are regarded as social outcasts yet are kind to others. Do you see what we are endeavouring to show, that the loving nature of the soul is the more important factor? But do not say that we have told you to be dishonest. All we are endeavouring to show is that the Master greatly valued loving kindness and forgiveness, and promised that in the following incarnation—or the next generation—the soul would receive a similar reward.

## *The Comforter*

&When we look out across the world and see the anguish and suffering of humankind, we know the great need there is for the Comforter. You, in common with all humanity, suffer loneliness and sickness; you suffer through the loss of something—what is it? The spirit, the fire, love. The companionship of the spirit. You suffer from separation and you too long for and wonder when the Comforter is coming. Who, then, is the Comforter? The Comforter is clearly described and revealed in the teachings of Jesus, the teachings of that Christ Spirit or the great White Light which has shone forth in varying degrees from the beginning of the world, its truth spoken through many of the great leaders and teachers of religion.

It would seem that in the Christian teaching, once it is understood by the western world, there is a clear, comprehensive outline of life. This reveals the nature of the soul and the human spirit, the purpose of reincarnation, the law of karma, the aspects of the psychic body, and psychic development. Crowning all, this outline reveals the Comforter, the Divine Light.

John the Baptist, anticipating Jesus' coming, spoke of baptism of fire: *I indeed baptize you with water ... but he shall baptize you with the Holy Ghost and with fire*—which is the magic light, the divine fire which falls from heaven, which is called the Holy Spirit. Thus a man, a woman, is born again. Although already born of the flesh and blood and water in his or her physical body, in the psychic body, in the soul body, he or she is not yet born from above, of the spirit, or the divine fire, until the divine baptism takes place.

Thus we see that there are two distinct aspects of the human being referred to again and again in parable, miracle, and in teaching by word: the soul, or the psychic aspect, and the spirit, the divine fire. Let us extricate one vital word, repeated again and again and yet again and seeming to be allied with the Christian spirit. This word is 'love'. Even love is not understood, because it has many aspects, many interpretations. The earnest and simple Christian however understands when Christ said, *Love one another.* So the Christian life is a striving to be loving.

## *The Future, and the Path of Perseverance*

❧The pathway up the mountainside to the heavenly summit is a long journey. Until an individual gets the first glimpse of the glory which awaits him or her, he or she is in travail on the planes of materialism. The individual enters into conflicts and wars, undergoes pain and sickness and separation, suffers misunderstanding, is subject to indignations, resentments, fears, anxieties and all the sorrows and ills that flesh is heir to. But it is not for you to wait until you are freed from the limitations of the flesh before you can realize happiness and your true being. For until you have learned to seek the innermost spirit while still living on the outermost material plane, you will not find that priceless jewel merely by discarding the physical body.

Do not let us mislead you. When you enter the spirit world, you will see a certain degree of God's love, and the true life that awaits you. Remember that this comes to the average soul when it has passed over, for then it is to a certain degree free enough to glimpse that the soul will do anything, suffer anything, dare anything, to know more. And so that soul will eventually ask its guardian angel (who is acting under the Lords of Karma) if it may return to earth, and to where it may return. For now the soul has now but one object, to develop its God-given quality, that it may expand in consciousness and know more of the glories it has glimpsed. Is this not natural?

When people dislike and reject the idea of reincarnation, they do not understand this great fullness, this allness of life, this at-one-ment. They are like snails in hard shells which they carry everywhere and do not want to discard. But when they lose their imprisoning shell, they want never to see it again and think that to come back would be retrogressive. That is because all around their soul body there is clinging the mud of materialism. But when the soul has learnt to cleanse self, when the soul has discarded this mud, it no longer thinks of life as a term of imprisonment. The soul knows that, whether on earth or in heaven, it is free, because the soul has shed that which is binding, and learnt to use those innermost powers that give freedom to every soul.

A glorious future lies before us all, but it means work—hard work. But hard work can be very interesting. Indeed the more interesting the job, the harder one will work, not realizing that it is work. For instance, if you have great love for music, and long to express your soul through some instrument, it is a joy to practise, to become proficient in the art. The same applies to all the arts and sciences; if you are wholly interested you do not mind work, nor the cost of attaining your object. So it is with this work of the soul.

To work upon the soul does not always demand the setting apart of long periods for meditation; but having decided upon your particular path, follow it steadfastly. Do not follow 'squirrel-tracks'; do not run hither and thither thinking that someone else has found a better path than yours and that you will try his or hers. As children when plucking flowers flit from patch to patch in case some other child has found better flowers than they, so do children of earth rush hither and thither after the truths of the spirit.

This is not the way. For a time will come when your innermost voice will speak to you, saying: 'This is my path; here I shall find peace. I will pursue this path, come what may'. Having made your decision, you must abide by it. You will not always find this easy; but if you persist and are patient, and above all never lose faith, your path will lead you unerringly to your goal.*

As you journey onwards, you seem to come up against life, people, conditions. Not only this, you come up against invisible forces that play upon your subtler bodies. Every experience you meet in every day life, in business or social relationships, or in your church or lodge, comes not accidentally but through a precise law. Life is governed by universal laws, two of which are those of reincarnation and karma. Therefore in each experience we have to look for the lesson presented by our guardian angel, our master, and the great Lords of

*This passage also occurs in White Eagle's SPIRITUAL UNFOLDMENT I.

Karma, which lesson will help us to unfold the inmost powers.

We see the hardships you are all enduring. The world is chaotic, not only because of wars, but because of the astral and etheric forces to which most of you react. You have finer bodies than you realize, and these thought-forces of passion and hatred and bloodshed are all beating upon your sensitive bodies and cause you nerve strain, heartache, sorrow, fear. This is your test—an opportunity for initiation. It does not come so potently in every incarnation, but in this age it is a special opportunity that is being presented to human-kind. Those who can understand and are ready to accept the challenge and work through it will indeed be blessed with a glorious reward. In future, do not let your thoughts dwell upon chaotic material conditions, but let your life be lived in the consciousness of the all-pervading spirit of the Father–Mother God—the Great White Spirit whom all we Indians worshipped and loved, from whom we drew our strength and sustenance for the spirit, and the blessings of material life.

God is omnipotent, omnipresent, omniscient; in God we live and have our being; and the purpose of life is to seek that universal religion or reunion with God. Thus shall we claim our son–daughtership with God, our brotherhood with all life, and with all cre-ated beings. Then we shall cease to prey upon any of the other beings on earth; then shall we live to give, to serve, to make happy all our human companions. This is true religion, unbounded by creed, dogma, race or time; for *as it was in the beginning, is now, and ever shall be; world without end. Amen.*

# References

ALL BIBLE quotations are from the King James Version, except 'Forgive us our trespasses' on p. 116, which is the Book of Common Prayer version. On p. 83, the quotation 'To thine own self be true' is from Shakespeare's *Hamlet*.